bracelets,
buttons
&
brooches

by Jane Davis

©2007 Jane Davis
Published by

kp krause publications
An Imprint of F+W Publications

700 East State Street • Iola, WI 54990-0001
715-445-2214 • 888-457-2873
www.krausebooks.com

Our toll-free number to place an order or obtain
a free catalog is (800) 258-0929.

The following registered trademark terms and companies appear in this publication:
JHB International®; Gita Maria®; Susan Clarke Originals©; Delica®; Nymo® Beading Thread; Clover Needlecraft, Inc.® Gold Eye Quilting Needle; Lacy's Stiff Stuff™; Toho™ One-G and C-Lon Beading Thread; Aleene's® Tacky Glue; LaMode® Buttons; Blue Moon Beads®; Creative Castle©; Swarovski®; Ultrasuede©

Library of Congress Control Number: 2007927492

ISBN 13: 978-0-89689-581-2
ISBN 10: 0-89689-581-5

Cover designed by Katrina Newby
Book Interior designed by Connie Biggar
Edited by Terri Dougherty

Printed in China

acknowledgments

This book has been a lot of fun to make. As always, I just wish I had more time to try out more ideas and spend time on variations for each project.

All the people at Krause Publications have been a joy to work with. Thank you to Susan Sliwicki for your help at the beginning stages of this project. Thank you to Terri Dougherty for your work at the editing stage. Your careful eye has brought this book together. A big thank you goes out to Candy Wiza at Krause Publications for saying yes to this idea, for being supportive and interested in my work, and for all the extra editing work you have done to get this book completed. Additional thanks to Katrina Newby, who designed the cover, Connie Biggar for the interior layout of the book, and Carole Tripp of Creative Castle in Newbury Park, California, for all your ideas and support, and especially for your friendship.

Finally, I'd like to thank my family for their understanding of deadlines and support of my many passions in arts and crafts. I couldn't do what I do without you.

table of contents

I have always been inspired by beautiful beaded-bezel cabochon beadwork, with its rich texture, smoothly polished stones and intricate beaded stitches. It also appeals to me to take something that wasn't meant to be a bead and incorporate it into a beaded piece by surrounding it with smaller beads to hold it in place. But bezel-encased stones are not the only thing that can be incorporated into beadwork. There are beautiful fused glass cabochons and an incredible variety of buttons, from modern to antiques to reproductions. Polymer clay that you buy or form yourself has an incredible range of bead-bezel-able possibilities. Also, larger beads that may have a hole in the wrong direction for your project, or that you just want to surround with smaller beads in your design, are great elements to add to your beadwork.

This book focuses on these aspects of beadwork, confining them to bracelets, buttons and brooches, all of which lend themselves to wonderful ways to make bead encasements. I've also tried to add a few interesting ideas on giving the projects a little something extra, such as a tiny photo shining through a transparent section of a fused glass cabochon, or a brooch with a favorite woodland scene hidden behind the face of a forest spirit.

Many of the projects in this book are for intermediate to advanced beaders, though some, such as the stickpins on page 94, are easy projects that beginning beaders can accomplish. And although there are no pendants or earring projects in the book, on page 27, I show you how to adapt the designs into other types of jewelry. I also suggest ideas at the beginning of many projects. My hope is that this book will be a useful source of projects and techniques for beading around objects and will be used both for making the projects and for creating unique creations of your own design.

—Jane Davis

basics

Here is a basic reference of the tools, materials and techniques you will need to complete the projects in this book. Some of the items and techniques listed are common to most areas of beadwork, while others are unique to beading around larger objects and/or making bracelets, buttons and brooches.

chapter one

tools & supplies

Following are descriptions of the tools and supplies you will need. Some of the projects in this book require specific supplies, such as the two-holed beads and Blue Moon buttons in the elastic-banded bracelet on page 70, or the five-holed spacers for the Egyptian bracelet on page 44. Other projects, such as the keepsake brooch on page 116, will be unique to you and will depend on the glass or stone you choose to incorporate into the design. This section is meant as a handy source to explain the tools and supplies used to make the projects, and how they pertain to the techniques used here.

Size 12 (small) and size 8 (large) cylinder beads

Cylinder

A cylinder bead is shaped like a cylinder and looks like a brick from the side. Cylinder beads come in two sizes, size 12 which is small, and size 8, large. The sizes correspond roughly to seed bead sizes. Cylinder beads are great for when you need a bead with a large hole, such as when stringing the elastic thread in the Silver and Black Elastic-Banded Bracelet on page 70, or making multiple passes through the beads, as in the Royal Blue Bracelet on page 30. They are also great for bordering the width of a thick stone, as with the Oriental Carving Bracelet on page 48.

Bugle

Bugle beads are elongated cylinder beads that can range from ¼" (0.6 cm) long to almost 2" (5 cm). They work great as anchors along an object with long straight sides, as in the Bugle Bead Abalone Bracelet on page 56.

Size 15 (smallest), 11 and 8 (largest) seed beads

Seed

A seed bead is basically shaped like a tall doughnut and comes in sizes ranging from almost a grain of salt, size 24 antique beads, to large size 5 pony beads, which are about ¼" (0.6 cm) across. The larger the bead size number, the smaller the bead. And hole size isn't tied to the bead size: you can have a large bead with a small hole, or a small bead with a fairly large hole. Generally speaking, Japanese-made beads, which are made by machine, are more consistent and have a larger hole than beads made by hand in other countries. Seed beads are the beads that you will use for the majority of projects in this book. Their rounded edges and variety of sizes make them ideal for hugging smoothly around the corners of cabochons or the curves of round and odd-shaped items.

Assorted bugle beads

Charlotte

Charlotte beads are seed beads that have a single facet ground on one side of the bead. They are made by hand, so the flat side is not consistent and some beads in a grouping are just plain seed beads. This variation causes them to randomly reflect light in beadwork.

Charlotte beads

Faceted

A faceted bead is any bead that has been ground flat on one or more sides. Swarovski crystals are one brand that contains 24 percent lead. Pearls, semiprecious stones, metal and wood beads are also available faceted. Faceted beads add sparkle to any project and come in many sizes and shapes.

Pearls and semiprecious stone beads

Pearls and Semiprecious

Pearls can be synthetic or natural, come in round or in many different shapes and can be dyed in a rainbow of colors. Semiprecious stone beads are available in a variety of shapes and sizes. They are great to coordinate with stone cabochons as in the Mini Stick Pins on page 94. I think pearls add a bit of elegance to any beading project.

Pressed Glass

Pressed glass is any bead that has been pressed into a mold to create a shape. The shapes can be simple or elaborate, from triangles to leaves and flowers. With the variety and subject matter used in pressed glass beads, you can create any feeling you choose when adding them to your projects.

Assorted faceted beads

Pressed glass

tools & supplies

Metal beads

Metal

Any bead made from metal, whether a base metal (tin, aluminum) or a precious metal (silver, gold), can be formed into just about any shape from spacers to large focal beads. Metal beads add a shine and texture to beadwork. Keep in mind that they also add weight to a piece, so when making a brooch or earrings you may want to limit the number of metal beads.

Combinations

Combinations

Beads can be made using more than one technique to create a more complex design. Pearls are sometimes faceted, or pressed glass beads are faceted on a section, leaving the rest of the bead showing the pressed shape.

Focal

A focal bead is the centerpiece of a design. It can be any large bead, usually with some significant design, and can be made of any material from polymer clay to glass or semi-precious stones.

Focal beads

Spacers and End Caps

A spacer is generally any bead that is significantly wider sideways than it is tall (through the hole). Most look like mini doughnut-shaped beads, but metal spacers can be very ornate. Multiple-hole spacers are long with the holes going through their sides at regular intervals, rather than one hole down the middle. They are great for separating strands of beads or helping with the structure of the piece, as in the Egyptian Stone Cylinders Bracelet on page 44. End caps are usually made of metal and are shaped like a small bowl so that they hug the bead they are next to. Spacer beads and end caps add detail and often a touch of color to strands of fringe or bracelets.

Spacers and end caps

Cabochons

Cabochons

Cabochons (also called cabs) are objects that have been shaped so that they are flat on the back side and rounded on the front. The rounded edge tapering to the flat back makes them ideal objects to bead around, creating a beveled setting while attaching them to a backing material. They can be ground from precious or semiprecious stones, or the shape can be made from many materials, including fused glass or polymer clay.

Buttons

Buttons

Buttons, old and new, are great items to incorporate into your beading. You have a choice between using an antique button or a new button which may or may not be a reproduction of an antique button. There are buttons with shanks (the back loop used to sew the button in place), and buttons with holes through the middle. Each causes you to choose how

to handle it in beadwork. For the shank buttons, you have to choose whether to keep the shank or cut it off. For buttons with holes in the middle, you need to decide whether to leave the holes as they are or add a little beading to cover them. In any case, buttons have an ever-growing variety of gorgeous designs to add detail to your beaded design.

Other focal objects

Other Focal Objects

Other than cabochons and buttons, what else can you bead around? Just about anything really, from shells to rocks, even beach glass and odd-shaped beads and stones. The trick is deciding on the beading method that best displays your item. A shell, for instance, might be beautiful beaded like a cabochon onto a backing material, but if it is as beautiful on the inside as on the outside, you might want to use peyote stitch and netting to make an open-backed setting so both sides are visible.

tools & supplies

Various sizes and colors of Nymo thread

Threads

There are several types of beading thread to choose from. You need to use a thread that is strong yet inconspicuous in your beadwork, and which you can pass through the bead holes as many times as you need to for your project. Nymo brands are probably the most common beading thread. It comes in many colors and sizes. For size 11 beads, size B or D is commonly used. One-G and C-Lon are two other commonly used brands of beading thread. I think that the thread you choose is a personal issue. Each beader has his or her favorite, so use the one that works best for you. I tend to use Nymo thread most of the time because of its availability and large range of colors.

Needles

Beading needles are long, thin needles with a long narrow eye. They come in sizes ranging from size 16 (the smallest) to size 9 (the largest). You will generally need a size 12 for most projects in this book. If you use size 15 beads or smaller, or beads with very small holes, you may need to use a smaller needle. For the elastic thread on the Silver and Black Elastic-Banded Bracelet, on page 70, you will need a needle with a hole large enough to thread the elastic, yet thin enough to pass through the cylinder beads. I used a Gold Eye Quilt Basting Needle, size 7. It was a challenge to thread the needle, but once done, I could finish the piece with ease.

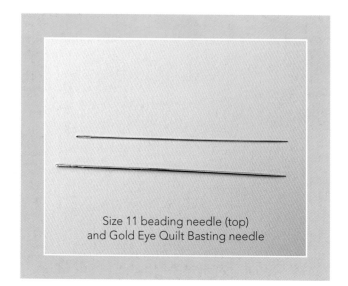

Size 11 beading needle (top)
and Gold Eye Quilt Basting needle

Fused interfacing (top), stiff interfacing, Lacy's Stiff Stuff

Backing Materials

Most of the projects in this book require attaching your beadwork to a backing material. You will generally need something to glue your cabochon to and sew beads to, and you will also need a decorative material to cover your stitches and finish the back side of the piece. The first material needs to be something that isn't flexible so that your large object won't slide out of its setting, but it also needs to be easy to sew through and not fray. Nonwoven interfacing will work, but isn't as firm as some other materials such as Lacy's Stiff Stuff, which is specifically made for cabochon beading. The final decorative backing most often used is leather or synthetic suede.

Beading Bases and Supports

When combining several beaded items in a piece, or if your beadwork extends more than ¼" (0.6 cm) beyond the perimeter of the cabochon, you will sometimes need to include something stiff to support the finished piece so it doesn't bend at weak points. This can be as simple as some stiff cardboard or plastic you cut to shape, a thin piece of wood, or metal flashing found at the hardware store. You will need to decide which type of material works best for your purpose. Each has its drawbacks: cardboard cannot get wet, wood is lightweight but is thicker than the others and metal is difficult to cut.

Cardboard and wood

Synthetic suede

Findings

Findings are the mechanics of your piece, from clasps and jump rings to pin backs and button backs. Clasps, especially, come in a huge variety, and you can chose from a locking clasp, a toggle clasp or a magnetic clasp, as well as clasps made from base metals or precious metals, all in basic or themed designs.

Sliderbar (left) and hook & eye clasps (above)

Jump rings (left) and pin back (right)

Decorative toggle clasp (left) and "S" hook clasp (right)

top to bottom:
bar pin
lobster claw clasp
stick pin blank
magnetic foldover clasp

Adhesives

There are basically two kinds of adhesives: those that are temporary and those that are made to be permanent. Both are used in this book. For adhering your object to the backing material, usually a thick white craft glue is all you will need. It doesn't need to be permanent, it just needs to hold the item in place as you bead. For anything that needs permanent adhesion, such as pin backs and button backs, you will need a strong permanent adhesive. Be sure to follow the directions carefully to get the strongest bond.

Other Tools

In addition to the already mentioned items, you will need a good pair of scissors with sharp points to cut the thread close to your beadwork, a place to bead with good lighting and a beading surface to lay out your beads while working, as well as a place to store your beads. You may want tools to help you see those tiny beads more clearly, such as reading glasses or magnifying lamps. For some of the projects you will need two sets of pliers to open and close jump rings, and if you choose to cut off the metal shanks of buttons for some of the projects you will need a strong pair of wire cutters.

Permanent glue (in tubes)
and temporary glue (in bottle)

Work area and tools

stitching techniques

This section illustrates the techniques you will need to complete the projects in this book. It is also a handy reference when you need to search for a technique for beading around objects on future projects of your own design.

Half-Hitch Knot

A half-hitch knot works well as an added anchor when weaving in the ends of the thread.

To make a half-hitch knot, take a small stitch in the backing material, or around one or two threads between beads, and pull almost all the way through so that a small loop still remains (Figure 1). Pass the needle through the loop and finish pulling the thread tight (Figure 2).

Figure 1   *Figure 2*

Square Knot

A square knot is a sturdy knot used as a beginning knot when working with backing material, and when tying two threads together.

To make a square knot, wrap one end of thread over, around and through the other piece of thread and pull tight (Figure 3). Then for the next step, wrap the thread that's in your other hand over, around, and through the other piece of thread (Figure 4). The mantra for this is "right over left, left over right." If you work the same direction for each knot, that is right over left, then right over left again, you will only have a granny knot, which will easily come undone.

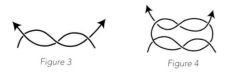

Figure 3   *Figure 4*

Quilter's Knot

This is a quick knot that I use often when beginning a thread that I plan to hide the knot in backing material. It takes some practicing at first, but it is an easy knot to make once you get the hang of it.

Thread the needle, then wrap the thread-tail around the needle about four times. Holding the wrapped part of the needle in one hand, pull the needle through, continuing to pinch the wrapped section of thread as you pull (Figure 5). The knot will tighten near the tail of the thread.

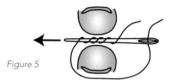

Figure 5

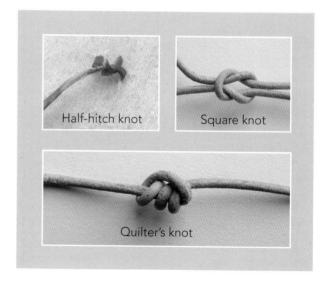

Half-hitch knot   Square knot

Quilter's knot

Beginning and Ending Threads

Beginning a thread with a backing material.

When beginning a thread on projects using a backing material that will be hidden in the final project, first tie a square knot or quilter's knot near the tail end of the thread and then come up through the backing material from the back to the front so that the tail and knot will be secured and hidden on the back side of the backing material (Figure 6).

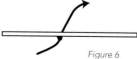

Figure 6

Beginning a thread in beadwork

When beginning a thread on beadwork projects that don't have a backing material, begin the work without a knot, leaving at least 8" (20 cm) of thread (Figure 7).

Ending a thread in beadwork

When you have worked some of the piece, thread the tail thread and weave the tail into the finished beadwork, passing back over the thread path several times so that the thread is locked in place, then cut the tail thread close to the beadwork. Use this same process for ending a thread (Figure 8).

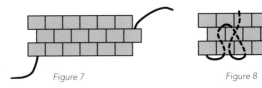

Figure 7   *Figure 8*

Backstitch

To make a backstitch with beads, come up from the back side of the backing material, *string two beads, pass back down through the backing material about two beads' width away (Figure 9). Then come back up through the backing material between the two beads and pass through the last bead strung (Figure 10 and 11). Repeat from asterisk. Backstitch with beads can be worked by stringing one or more beads at a time. I like to work with no more than three beads, as I feel this makes a sturdier row of beads, though you can make a backstitch with any number of beads.

Running Stitch

To make a running stitch with beads, come up from the back side of the backing material, *string one bead, pass back down through the backing material about one bead's width away (Figure 12). Then come back up through the backing material one bead's width away (Figure 13). Repeat from the asterisk.

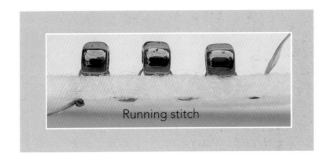

Running stitch

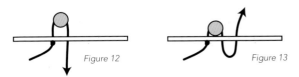

Figure 12   *Figure 13*

Passing Through the Outer Beads

After you have made an edging around your cabochon, you may need to travel with the thread to a different section on your beaded piece. To do this, follow the thread path already established, weaving in and out of the beads to get to your desired location (Figure 14).

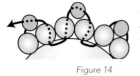

Figure 14

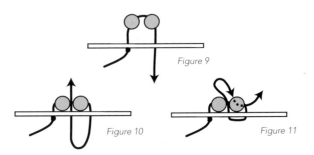

Figure 9

Figure 10   *Figure 11*

stitching techniques

Peyote Stitch

Peyote stitch on backing material

There are two ways to begin peyote stitch on backing material. One way is to work a row of beaded running stitch on the backing material. Then for the second row, simply string one bead then pass through the next bead on the backing material, repeating across the row (Figure 15). The other way is to work backstitch, placing the beads right next to each other. You've just completed the first two rows. Now you string one bead, skip one bead on the backing material, then pass through the next bead on the backing material, and repeat across (Figure 16).

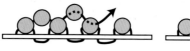

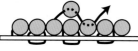

Figure 15   Figure 16

Free-standing peyote stitch

To work peyote stitch without a backing fabric, you string the number of beads that you will need for the first and second rows. Then, beginning the third row, string one bead, then pass back through the third bead from the needle (Figure 17). *String one bead, skip one bead on the strand, pass through the next bead (Figure 18). Repeat from asterisk to the end of the row. If you have an even number of beads in each row, you will be able to begin each row as in Figure 17. If you have an odd number of beads in the row you will need to weave in and out of the beads to position the thread for the first bead in the next row (Figure 19).

Figure 17

 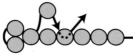

Figure 18   Figure 19

Netting Stitch

Netting stitch is a flexible open stitch that is great for working around objects. It is actually closely related in structure to peyote stitch in that each row is made by working in the previous row and is half a stitch off from the previous row's stitches. Netting stitch can be worked using any number of beads in each stitch, except for just one bead, because then it is peyote stitch. The projects in this book use three-bead netting stitch.

To work three-bead netting stitch continuing off of peyote stitch around a cabochon, work several rows of peyote stitch, then *string three beads, skip the next bead of the previous row and pass through the next bead of the previous row (Figure 20). Repeat from the asterisk around. When you reach the beginning, pass through two beads of the first netting stitch (Figure 21). For the next row, **string three beads, pass through the second bead of the next three-bead group from the previous row (Figure 22). Repeat from double asterisk. When you reach the beginning, pass through two beads of the first netting stitch. Repeat from double asterisk for each row. Close the netting around the cabochon by changing to smaller beads after several rows. For the final row, use only two beads for each stitch, then pass through the beads several times to snug up the beads and thread. Weave in ends.

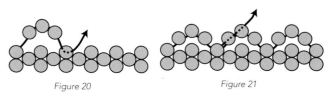

Figure 20   Figure 21

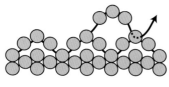

Figure 22

Ladder Stitch

Ladder stitch is the beginning row of brick stitch, but it is also used alone or in combination with many other techniques.

Ladder stitch can be worked with one thread, threaded with a needle at both ends, or it can be worked with one thread and one needle. To make a ladder stitch with two needles, string two beads onto one needle and slide

them to the middle of the thread. Pass the other needle through the second bead strung, and pull tightly (Figure 23). The beads will sit one on top of the other. *String one bead with one needle, pass the other needle through the bead (Figure 24). Repeat from asterisk until the strip is as long as you need.

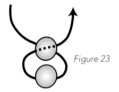
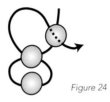

Figure 23

Figure 24

Brick Stitch

Continuing with the ladder stitch piece you made above, remove one of the needles. With the remaining needle pass through the second bead on the strip (Figure 25),

Brick stitch

string two beads, pass through the thread between the last two beads on the ladder stitch strip, pass up through the second bead strung (Figure 26). String one bead, pass through the thread between the second and third beads on

the ladder stitch strip, pass through the bead just strung (Figure 27). *String one bead, pass through the thread between the third and fourth beads on the ladder stitch strip, pass through the bead just strung. Repeat from asterisk, working between the fourth and fifth beads, then fifth and sixth and so on. At the end of the row pass down through the row before and up through the second bead in the current row then repeat the two-bead start for the next row.

Fringe

Fringe is made up of a grouping of single dangles of beads. Any combination of beads will make a fringe, but often a larger bead or beads are placed near the end of the length of beads, giving the dangle added weight and causing it to hang gracefully.

To make fringe, begin with your thread coming out where you want your fringe to begin, or begin at the middle of your desired fringe and work out in one direction, then in the other direction. String the beads for one dangle. The last bead or beads you string will be your turnaround bead(s). Skip these last beads and pass back up through the beads you just strung, back up to the beadwork piece (Figure 28). To make sure that you haven't pierced the thread already in the bead holes, before you pull your needle through the beads, pull toward you for a few inches, sliding the beads with the needle to be sure they slide smoothly. Pull the needle through, hold on to the turnaround beads with your other hand and tighten the beads and thread so the beads sit snugly together and the turnaround beads fit next to the rest of the beads. Pass up through the beads in your beadwork and out where you want the next dangle to begin. If the beads along the edge are small and you don't think they will be able to support the weight of each individual dangle, pass up several rows of beadwork before working your way down to begin the next dangle. This way your fringe won't be hanging from just one bead, but from several within the piece. Work each dangle in this way.

Figure 28

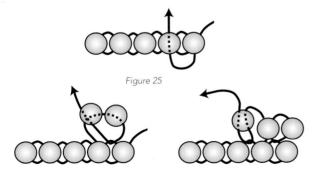

Figure 25

Figure 26

Figure 27

Here are several basic ways to bead around your cabochon or chosen large object. Keep in mind that a lot depends on the shape of what you are actually beading around. The thickness and curve of the piece from the edge to the top will often dictate what size bead to begin with and how many rows of beads you need to get your bezel to hold the piece in place. The size and uniformity of your smaller beads will also have an effect on how many beads you use and how everything fits together. You will find that sometimes you will need to take a row out and redo it, adjusting the number of beads to fit your piece. Generally speaking, if you want to work with just two rows of beads to hold your cabochon in place, you need your first row of beads to be almost the height of your cabochon, and the second row to be a smaller size bead. When working several rows to make the bezel you can use large or small beads, but beginning with larger beads and then changing to smaller beads after a few rows makes an easy, graduated, smooth decrease.

Creating a Bezel Setting Using Backing and Backstitch

To make a bezel setting using backing material and backstitch, you will need your cabochon, a piece of backing material approximately ¼" (0.6 cm) larger than the stone on all sides, a beading needle and beading thread, and two sizes of beads, one as large or almost as large as the height of the stone and one size smaller, and some thick white glue.

Step 1 - Stitching the base row

Using a small amount of glue, glue your cab to the center of the backing material. Let dry. Thread a 40" (102 cm) length of thread with the beading needle and tie a knot near the tail. Come up from the back of the backing material close to the cab. *Using the larger beads, string two beads and enter the backing material about two beads' width away, next to the cab (Figure 1). Pass back up through the backing material between the two beads, pass through the last bead strung (Figure 2). Repeat from asterisk around the cab. Pass through the beads several times to tighten the beads snugly around the cab. Pass down through the backing material.

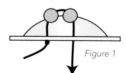
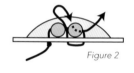

Figure 1   Figure 2

Step 2 - Stitching the bezel row

Pass up through the backing material between the cab and the row of larger beads. *Using the smaller seed beads, string two beads and enter the backing material about two beads' width away, between the cab and the larger beads (Figure 3). Keep the tension loose enough so the smaller row of beads sits above the first row, next to the cab, rather than sinking down to the backing material. Pass back up through the backing material between the two beads, pass through the last bead strung (Figure 4). Repeat from asterisk around the cab. Pass through the beads several times to tighten the beads snugly around the cab. Pass down through the backing material.

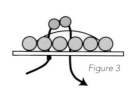
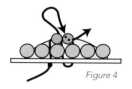

Figure 3   Figure 4

Creating a Bezel Setting Using a Backing and Tubular Peyote Stitch

To make a bezel setting using backing material and peyote stitch, you will need your cabochon, a piece of backing material approximately ¼" (0.6 cm) larger than the stone on all sides, a beading needle and beading thread, and two sizes of beads, generally size 11 and size 15, and some thick white glue.

Step 1 - The base row in running stitch

Using a small amount of glue, glue your cab to the center of the backing material. Let dry. Thread a 40" (102 cm) length of thread with the beading needle and tie a knot near the tail. Come up from the back of the backing material close to the cab. *Using the larger beads string one bead and enter the backing material about a bead's width away, next to the cab. Pass back up through the backing material one bead's width away (Figure 5). Repeat from asterisk around the cab, making sure there is a space between the last bead and the first bead in the round.

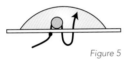

Figure 5

Step 2 - Row 2

Pass through the first bead strung (Figure 6). **String one bead, pass through the next bead of the previous row (Figure 7). Repeat from double asterisks around.

Figure 6   *Figure 7*

Step 3 - Remaining rows

Pass through the next bead (Figure 8). Repeat from the double asterisk in step 2 for each row, changing to the smaller beads after a few rows to close the beads around the cab. Pass through the last row several times to tighten the beads snugly around the cab. Weave in the ends.

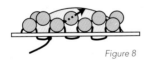

Figure 8

Creating a Bezel Setting Using a Backing and Classic Edging Stitch

To make a bezel setting using backing material and a classic edging stitch, you will need your cabochon, a piece of backing material approximately ¼" (0.6 cm) larger than the stone on all sides, a beading needle and beading thread, and two sizes of beads, one as large or almost as large as the height of the stone and one size smaller, and some thick white glue.

Step 1 - Stitching the base row and part of the bezel row

Using a small amount of glue, glue your cab to the center of the backing material. Let dry. Thread a 40" (102 cm) length of thread with the beading needle and tie a knot near the tail. Come up from the back of the backing material close to the cab. String one large bead, one small bead, and one large bead. Enter the backing material about one large bead's width away, next to the cab (Figure 9). *Pass back up through the backing material about one large bead's width away, string one large bead, one small bead, and one large bead, then pass back down through the backing material another large bead's width away (Figure 10a). Repeat from asterisk around the cab. At the end of the row, **pass up through the next large bead, string one small bead, and working in the opposite direction, pass down through the next large bead (Figure10b). Repeat from double asterisks, adding a small bead between the large beads that don't have one between them. Add a small bead between each three-bead set.

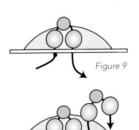

Figure 9

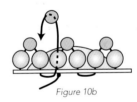

Figure 10a   *Figure 10b*

Step 2 - Closing the bezel row around the cab

Pass up through the first two beads again (Figure 11). *String one small bead and pass through the small bead of the next three-bead set (Figure 12). Repeat from asterisk around the cab. You may need to re-string this round a few times, omitting or adding a bead occasionally, to get the correct number of beads so they fit snugly together. Pass through the beads you added and string through several times to tighten them together so they hold the cab in place. Pass back down through the backing material.

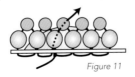 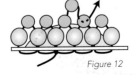

Figure 11   *Figure 12*

encasing your accent bead or object

*String one size 15 bead, one size 11 bead, one size 15 bead and pass through the next cylinder bead (Figure 13). Repeat on the other side of the ladder stitch beads (Figure 14a). Repeat from asterisk around, then stitch around again, passing through the size 15 beads and adding a size 11 bead between the beginning and end of each three-bead set (Figure 14b). There will be three beads sitting between each cylinder on the top and the bottom of the ladder stitch circle. Pass up through the next size 15 and 11 bead. Now, slide the beadwork over the object and close the size 11 beads into a tight circle around the top of the object by adding a size 11 bead every few beads so that the top closes tightly together with no gaps of thread (Figure 15). You may need to string this row several times to get the right placement and number of beads to fit evenly. Repeat on the other side of the ladder stitch beads and weave in ends.

Creating an Open-backed Enclosure With Ladder and Peyote Stitches

Encasing an object so that the back and front both show is a matter of stitching beads around the perimeter of the piece, then decreasing on one side and then the other, so that the piece is held in place. The easiest type of piece to stitch in this technique is something that is level and has sides about as thick as the large cylinder beads.

You will need 3.3 mm or size 8 cylinder beads, size 11 and 15 seed beads and a beading needle and thread. Using a 40" (102 cm) length of thread and the cylinder beads, make a ladder stitch strip that fits snugly around the object. Close it into a circle by passing through the first and last beads and tying the working thread and tail into a square knot. Slide the ladder stitch circle onto the object you are using to make sure it fits, then remove it from the object while stitching the following rows.

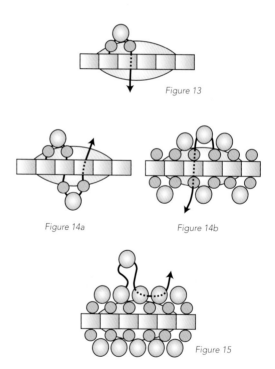

Figure 13

Figure 14a

Figure 14b

Figure 15

Creating an Open-backed Enclosure With Peyote and Netting Stitches

You will need beads in two sizes, generally size 11 and size 15 beads, your cabochon, beading needle and thread.

Using a 40" (102 cm) length of thread and the larger beads, string enough beads to fit the circumference of the cab. Take off one or two beads, then pass through the beads again to make a circle. This will provide a tight-fitting band of beadwork around your cab. Tie the tail and working thread into a square knot (Figure 16).

Figure 16

Work two rounds of peyote stitch, then slide the ring around the cab to see if it fits (Figure 17). Rework the ring if necessary to get a close fit. *Using the smaller beads, work two or three rounds of netting, stitching the first round through every other bead of the previous peyote stitch row (Figure 18). For the final round, string two beads for each set of beads instead of three, or any number needed to get a snug fit. Pass through this round several times to tighten it close to the cab. Repeat from asterisk on the other side of peyote stitch band, closing the beading around the cab.

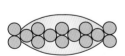

Figure 17

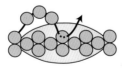

Figure 18

encasing your accent bead or object

Creating an Open-backed Enclosure for Square Shapes

You will need beads in two sizes, generally size 11 and size 15 beads, a flat square shape at least as thick as the larger beads, a tape measure, beading thread and a beading needle.

Measure one side of your square shape. *String enough size 11 beads to measure half the length of one side of the square shape. String the same length of the smaller beads. Repeat from the asterisk three more times. **Pass through the size 11 beads, string the same number of smaller beads as before (Figure 19). Repeat from the double asterisks three more times. Tie the tail and working thread into a tight square knot (Figure 20). Slide the corners of the square shape between the sets of smaller beads (Figure 21). You may need to restring the beads several times to get the correct number of beads for your piece to fit snugly with no gaps of thread showing.

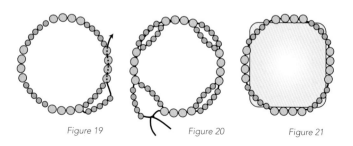

Figure 19   Figure 20   Figure 21

Finishing Beaded Cabochons With Synthetic Suede Backing

Cut the backing material close to the finished beadwork. Cut a piece of suede to the same size. Glue the suede to the backing material in the center only, using a very small amount of glue, just enough to hold it in place. Let dry. Thread a 24" (61 cm) length of thread with the beading needle and tie a knot at the tail end. Make a small stitch in the backing material to anchor the thread and hide the tail between the backing material and the suede. String two beads, make a small stitch through the suede and backing material and pass back through the last bead strung (Figure 22). *String one bead, make a small stitch through the suede and backing material about one bead's width away and pass back through the last bead strung (Figure 23). Repeat from asterisk around. When you get near the beginning, space your stitches so you will end up with no gaps in the beadwork. For the last stitch, pass down through the first bead strung (Figure 24). Take a small stitch in the suede and weave in the thread.

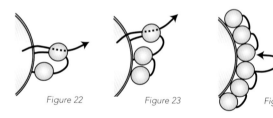

Figure 22   Figure 23   Figure 24

Opening and Closing Jump Rings

Jump rings come in handy for lengthening bracelets and necklaces, for attaching sections of beadwork together, and for making earrings.

It's important to open and close jump rings by rotating the ends away from each other rather than pulling them apart, so that you maintain the shape of the ring (Figure 25). Use two pliers and gently pull one end toward you and push the other away from you to open the ring, slide the beadwork or links onto the jump ring, then close it in the same manner (Figure 26).

Figure 25　　　　　　　*Figure 26*

Not Just Bracelets, Buttons and Brooches - How to Make Earrings and Pendants, Too

Many of the bead-encased components for projects in this book can easily be made into earrings or pendants to go with the finished project. You can also make an earring set or pendants instead of the project.

To make your project into a pendant or a set of earrings, don't cut the working thread when you have finished beading your item. Instead, weave through the outer beads until you reach the end you want to be the top of the pendant or earring. String a small loop of beads, about five size 15 beads (Figure 27), or sew a jump ring in place by passing through the ring and adjacent beads on the component several times (Figure 28). Weave in the end and attach one or two additional jump rings. The last jump ring for a pendant needs to be large enough to thread onto a chain. On the last jump ring you add to an earring, slide the earring finding onto the jump ring before closing it. Be sure to make another earring if you want a set!

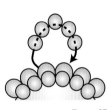
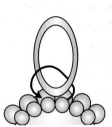

Figure 27　　　　　　*Figure 28*

bracelets

This collection of bracelet ideas varies from a simple beaded cabochon on a peyote stitch band to an interesting encasement of a flat square of abalone. For all the projects, you first work the focal beadwork, then string or bead the strap of the bracelet. For more bracelets, look in the first part of the Buttons chapter, page 60, to see several ideas for making bracelets with buttons.

chapter two

Alternating embellished beads with unadorned beads shows the transformation which has taken place in this embellished bead bracelet. This sparkly bracelet can be made with just about any 8 mm bead, though the faceted beads created the sparkle in the sample. You create the possibilities with your choice of beads and colors, making a bracelet that can go just as easily with blue jeans as it does with a dress.

MATERIALS

8 dark blue 8 mm faceted beads
18 silver spacer beads
11 to 15 blue Swarovski crystal 4 mm faceted beads
4 g iridescent blue size 12 cylinder beads
4 g blue size 15 seed beads
Size B beading thread
Size 12 beading needle
Clasp

Embellished 8 mm Bead (make five)

Step 1
Making the cylinder bead circle and attaching it to the 8 mm bead

Using the cylinder beads and a 30" (76 cm) length of thread make a two-bead-wide peyote stitch strip using 32 beads, or whatever multiple of four beads you need to fit snugly around your 8 mm bead (Figure 1). Pass through the beginning beads as shown (Figure 2), and tie a square knot with the beginning and ending threads (Figure 3).

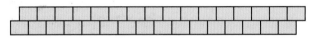

Figure 1

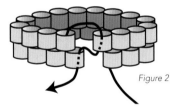

Figure 2

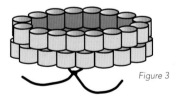

Figure 3

Step 2

Pass through one cylinder bead to the center of the two columns of beads (Figure 4). Position the cylinder beads around an 8 mm bead so the working thread is near one end of the 8 mm bead hole, then pass the needle through the 8 mm bead and through the center of the peyote stitch strip on the opposite side (Figure 5). Pass through two cylinder beads (Figure 6), then back down through the 8 mm bead again and out through the center of the peyote strip on the first side. Pass through one cylinder bead to the edge of the peyote strip (Figure 7).

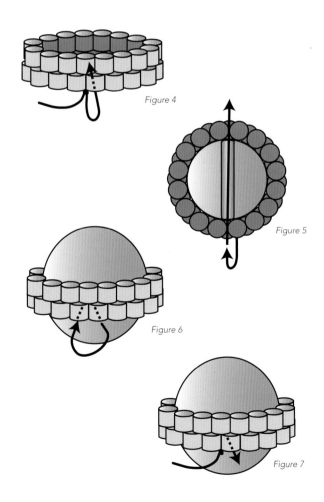

Figure 4

Figure 5

Figure 6

Figure 7

Step 3
Embellishing the cylinder bead circle with size 15 seed beads

*String three size 15 seed beads. Pass diagonally up through two cylinder beads, string three size 15 seed beads then pass diagonally down through the next two cylinder beads (Figure 8). Repeat from asterisk around the peyote strip.

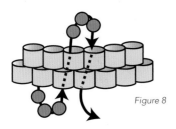

Figure 8

Step 4

*String five size 15 seed beads. Pass diagonally down through the cylinder beads (Figure 9). Repeat from asterisk around the peyote strip. Weave in ends.

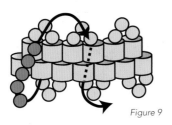

Figure 9

Stringing the Bracelet

Thread the needle with a 40" (102 cm) length of thread and pull through so it is doubled. Pass through one end of the clasp and tie a square knot, leaving a 6" (15 cm) tail to weave in later. String one size 15 seed bead, one crystal, *one spacer, one crystal, one spacer, one 8 mm bead, one spacer, one crystal, one spacer, one embellished 8 mm bead. Repeat two more times from *. String one spacer, one crystal, one spacer, one 8 mm bead. Repeat from **. String one spacer, one crystal, once spacer. String a repeat of one size 15 seed bead and one crystal until the bracelet will be the desired length when the end of the clasp is added. String one size 15 seed bead, then pass through the clasp and back through all the beads to the other end of the clasp. Knot the end to the clasp and weave in the ends.

cabochons bracelet

Finished size: approx. 7½" (19 cm) to 8" (20 cm) long
Skill level: Intermediate

This is a great project to try out several ways for beading cabochons. The central piece is worked in classic edging stitch, while the side triangle shapes are beaded in backstitch. You don't have to have the same shaped cabochons to make a nice bracelet. You could use several oval shapes, or even skip the strap and link six or seven small beaded cabochons together for an interesting cuff design.

MATERIALS

Purple oval cabochon approx. 13 mm tall
2 purple tapered cabochons approx. 13 mm x 19 mm
4 gray-blue 6 mm round faceted pearls
2 transparent lavender 6 mm oval faceted beads
16 medium-purple 5 mm wide faceted spacer beads
4 g dark-purple size 11 seed beads
4 g dark-purple size 15 seed beads
4 g light-purple size 15 seed beads
4 g silver-colored size 12 charlotte beads
12 silver 3 mm spacer beads
3 scraps of backing material, each ¼" (0.6 cm) larger on all sides than the cabs
3 scraps of suede, each about ⅛" (0.3 cm) larger on all sides than the beaded cabs
Size B beading thread
Size 12 beading needle
Clasp
Thick white glue
Optional: Gita Maria heart shape #CH006CP01
Charm
Jump rings
Pliers

Beading Around the Central Oval Cabochon

Step 1 *Stitching the base row and part of the bezel row*

Using a small amount of glue, glue your cab to the center of the backing material. Let dry. Thread a 40" (102 cm) length of thread with the beading needle and tie a knot near the tail. Come up from the back of the backing material close to the cab. Using the dark-purple size 15 seed beads, string three beads and enter the backing material about one bead's width away, next to the cab (Figure 1). *Pass back up through the backing material about one bead's width away, string three beads and pass back down through the backing material another bead's width away (Figure 2). Repeat from asterisk around the cab.

Step 2 *Closing the bezel row around the cab*

Pass up through the first two size 15 beads again (Figure 3). *String one bead and pass through the center bead of the next three-bead set (Figure 4). Repeat from asterisk around the cab, but several times don't add a bead, just pass through the center bead of the next three-bead set, so that the existing beads pull together to hold the cab in place (Figure 5). You may need to re-string this round a few times to get the correct number of beads so they fit snugly together. Pass through the beads you added and string through several times to tighten them together so they hold the cab in place. Pass back down through the backing material.

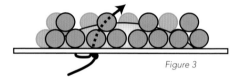

Figure 3

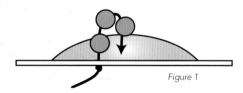

Figure 1

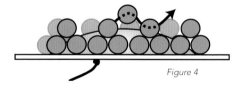

Figure 4

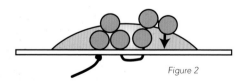

Figure 2

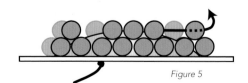

Figure 5

Step 3 *Adding another row of beads around the bezel row*

Pass up through the backing material and through one of the beads closest to the backing material. Working only through the beads that are closest to the backing material with their holes pointed up, string one size 15 bead and pass back down through the next bead (Figure 6). *Pass up through the next bead, string one bead and pass down through the next bead (Figure 7). Repeat from asterisk around the cab, passing up through the first two beads when you've stitched all the way around (Figure 8). Add a bead between each bead you've just added by stringing a bead, then passing through the next bead on the top row (Figure 9). Pass through this outer round of beads several times. Weave in thread ends.

Step 4 *Finishing with the suede backing*

Cut the backing material close to the finished beadwork. Cut a piece of suede to the same size. Glue the suede to the backing material in the center only, using a very small amount of glue, just enough to hold it in place. Let dry. Thread a 24" (61 cm) length of thread with the beading needle and tie a knot at the tail end. Make a small stitch in the backing material to anchor the thread and hide the tail between the backing material and the suede. String one silver charlotte, one size 15 light-purple bead and one silver charlotte, make a small stitch through the suede and backing material and pass back through the last bead strung (Figure 10). *String one size 15 light-purple bead and one silver charlotte, make a small stitch through the suede and backing material about one bead's width away and pass back through the silver charlotte (Figure 11). Repeat from asterisk around. When you get near the beginning, space your stitches so you will end up with no gaps in the beadwork. For the last stitch, string one light-purple size 15 bead and pass down through the first silver charlotte that you strung (Figure 12). Take a small stitch in the suede and weave in the thread.

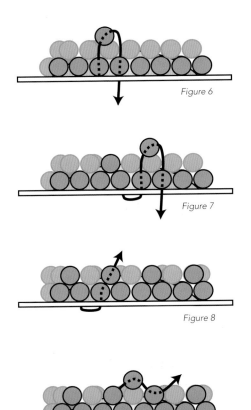

Figure 6

Figure 7

Figure 8

Figure 9

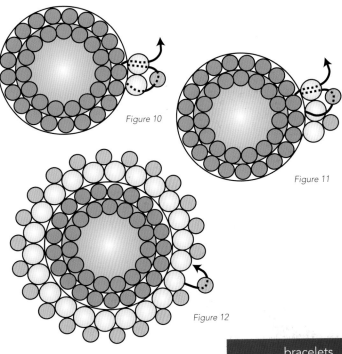

Figure 10

Figure 11

Figure 12

Beading Around the Tapered Cabochons (make two)

Step 1 *Stitching the base row*

Using a small amount of glue, glue your cab to the center of the backing material. Let dry. Thread a 40" (102 cm) length of thread with the beading needle and tie a knot near the tail. Come up from the back of the backing material close to the cab. *Using the dark-purple size 11 seed beads string two beads and enter the backing material about two beads' width away, next to the cab (Figure 13). Pass back up through the backing material between the two beads, pass through the last bead strung (Figure 14). Repeat from asterisk around the cab. Pass through the beads several times to tighten the beads snugly around the cab. Pass down through the backing material.

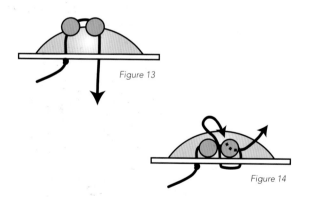

Figure 13

Figure 14

Step 2 *Stitching the bezel row*

Pass up through the backing material between the cab and the row of size 11 beads. *Using the dark-purple size 15 seed beads string two beads and enter the backing material about two beads' width away, between the cab and the size 11 beads (Figure 15). Pass back up through the backing material between the two beads, pass through the last bead strung (Figure 16). Repeat from asterisk around the cab. Pass through the beads several times to tighten the beads snugly around the cab. Pass down through the backing material.

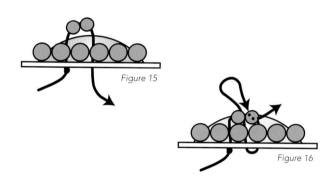

Figure 15

Figure 16

Step 3
Finishing the edge and attaching the cabs

Finish with the suede backing and edge beading design following the instructions in step 4 for the oval cab, except do not end the thread. When you have finished the edging, pass through the outer beads until your thread is coming out at the larger end of the tapered shape. You will be adding two rows of beads, so have your thread coming out a little off center along the edge, and coming out of a charlotte bead. *String one light-purple size 15 seed bead, one size 11 seed bead, one faceted spacer bead, one size 11 seed bead, and one light-purple size 15 seed bead. Pass through a charlotte bead on the oval cab and take a small stitch in the backing material, then back out the charlotte. Pass back through the beads you have strung and through the charlotte bead on the tapered cab.* String in and out of the beads on the tapered cab until you are coming out of a charlotte several beads away. Repeat the steps between the asterisks to make the other strand of beads connecting the two cabs together. Repeat step 3, attaching the remaining tapered cab to the other side of the oval cab. Weave in ends.

Stringing the Bracelet

Thread the needle with a 24" (61 cm) strand of thread and anchor it in the small end of one of the tapered cabs so that the thread is coming out of one of the light-purple size 15 seed beads at the center of the end of the cab. String one charlotte, one silver spacer, one faceted spacer, one pearl, one faceted spacer, one silver spacer, one charlotte, one silver spacer, one faceted spacer, one faceted transparent bead, one faceted spacer, one silver spacer, one charlotte, one silver spacer, one faceted spacer, one pearl, one faceted spacer, one silver spacer, one charlotte, and one end of the clasp. Pass back through all the beads strung and through the light-purple size 15 seed bead on the cab, entering it in the opposite direction from which the thread originally came out. Pass through several beads on the edge of the tapered cab, then back through the strung beads and through the clasp. Tie a knot around the clasp and pass back through at least 1" (2.5 cm) of the strung beads. Cut the thread close to the beads. Repeat the process on the end of the other tapered cab, using the other part of the clasp.

Optional Charm Dangle

Using the pliers, connect the heart shape and charm to the looped end of the bracelet with three jump rings between the bracelet and the heart, and one jump ring between the heart and the charm.

This delicate little design is quick and fun to make. The silver theme will work with many stone colors, and any that wouldn't work would probably look great with gold tones. The small elements can also be used for wonderful earrings to match your bracelet. You will need pairs of cabochons that are almost the same size to make each link, although they don't have to be small ovals. Round cabochons would give the piece a different look. However, free-form cabs or triangle shapes would be difficult to match up.

MATERIALS

6 small turquoise cabochons approx. 4 mm x 6 mm
6 Swarovski crystals 8 mm to match cabochons
4 g silver-colored size 11 charlottes
4 g silver-colored size 15 seed beads
12 silver end caps
6 or more silver 3 mm spacer beads (A)
Approx. 4 silver 3 mm spacer beads (in a different design) (B)
Size B beading thread
Size 12 beading needle
3 squares of backing material, ½" (1.3 cm)
Thick white glue
Clasp

Double-sided Beaded Cabochon (make three)

Step 1 *Stitching the base rows and part of the bezel rows*

Using a small amount of glue, glue a cabochon to each side of the backing material pieces, being careful to make sure they are centered over each other (Figure 1). Set aside to dry. Thread a 30" (76 cm) length of thread with the beading needle and tie a knot near the tail, leaving at least a 12" (30 cm) tail to use later to string the bracelet together. Come up from one side of the backing material close to the cabs. *Using the size 15 seed beads, string three beads and enter the backing material about one bead's width away, working close to the cabs (Figure 2). String three beads and pass back up through the backing material one bead's width away from the beads on the other side of the backing material (Figure 3). Repeat from asterisk around the cab, ending the round by coming up through the first bead strung (Figure 4).

Step 2 *Closing the bezel row around the cab*

Working in the opposite direction *string one size 15 bead, then pass through the next bead, through the backing material, and out through the bead on the other side of the backing material (Figure 5). Repeat from the asterisk until there is a bead between all the beads stitched to the backing material. Pass through the next bead, string one bead and pass through the next bead. Repeat this around, only adding beads as needed to fill the space between beads, yet add enough to close the circle of beads so they hold the cab in place. You may have to re-string this round several times until you get a snug-fitting circle with no gaps. Pass through this circle of beads several times to tighten the beads snugly around the cab. Pass down through the backing material and repeat from the asterisk for the cab on the other side of the piece. Do not weave in the ends. Pass the thread down through the backing material and out to the edge of the piece.

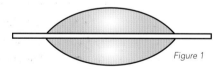

Figure 1

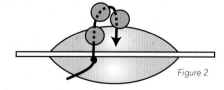

Figure 2

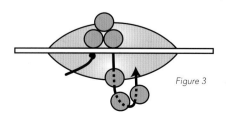

Figure 3

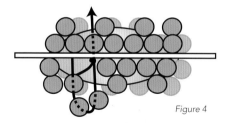

Figure 4

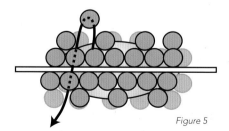

Figure 5

Step 3
Adding the edging around the cab

String one charlotte, one size 15 bead and one charlotte, make a small stitch through the backing material and pass back through the last bead strung (Figure 6). *String one size 15 bead and one charlotte, make a small stitch through the backing material between the next two beads and pass back through the charlotte (Figure 7). Repeat from asterisk around. For the last stitch, string one size 15 bead and pass down through the first charlotte strung (Figure 8).

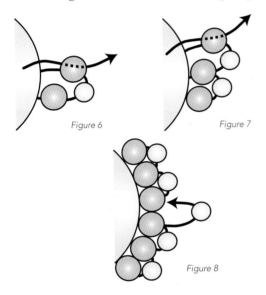

Figure 6

Figure 7

Figure 8

Step 4
Attaching the three-beaded cabs together

*Continuing with the working thread from step 3, pass through the outer beads until the thread is coming out a bead at one end of the oval-shaped piece. If the thread is coming out of a charlotte, string one size 15 bead. String one charlotte, one end cap, one crystal, one end cap and one charlotte. Pass through a bead on one of the other beaded cabs, then pass through several beads on that cab before passing back through the beads you strung to the first beaded cab. Weave in the end. Repeat from the asterisk for the third beaded cab, attaching it to the other side of the center-beaded cab. Weave in the ends of the center-beaded cab and the ends that you used to attach the cabs together.

Stringing the Bracelet

There will be two threads left, one on each outer-beaded cab. Working with one of these, *pass through the outer beads of the cab so that the thread is coming out of a bead at the remaining end of the cab. String one size 15 seed bead if the thread is coming out of a charlotte. String one charlotte, one end cap, one crystal, one end cap, one charlotte, one spacer (A), one charlotte, one spacer (B), one charlotte, one spacer (A) , one charlotte, one end cap, one crystal, one end cap, one charlotte, one spacer (B), one charlotte, one spacer (A), one charlotte. Pass through one end of the clasp and back through all the beads to beaded cab. Pass through several beads on the beaded cab, then pass back through all the strung beads to the clasp. Tie a knot to the clasp and pass back through at least 1" (2.5 cm) of the strung beads. Cut the thread close to the beads. Repeat from asterisk for the other end of the bracelet, adding more or fewer beads to adjust the size of the bracelet to fit.

egyptian stone cylinders bracelet

This design is dependent on the shape of the stones and the multiple-holed spacer beads and bar clasp for its cuff-like look.

MATERIALS

5 agate stone cylinders, approx. 3 mm diameter by 25 mm long
4 g gold-toned size 11 seed beads
4 g gold-toned size 15 seed beads
4 g black size 15 seed beads
6 gold-toned size 1 bugle beads
6 black 8 mm bicone beads
6 black 4 mm fire-polished beads
24 black 3 mm x 5 mm faceted rondelle beads
44 black 3 mm fire-polished beads
48 druk 3 mm beads to match the stone agate colors
6 gold-toned 4 mm fire-polished beads
2 three-hole spacer bars
2 five-hole spacer bars
Size B beading thread
Size 12 beading needle
Sliding bar clasp with three ring attachments

Encasing the Stone Beads (make five)

Step 1 *Peyote stitch caps*

Using a 24" (61 cm) length of thread and the size 11 gold beads, string three beads, pass through them again to form a circle. Tie the tail and working thread into a square knot (Figure 1). Pass through one bead next to the knot, *string two black size 15 beads, pass through the next bead (Figure 2). Repeat from the asterisk twice more. Pass through the first bead of the next two-bead set, **string one bead and pass through the second bead of the same two-bead set (Figure 3). String one bead and pass through the first bead of the next two-bead set (Figure 4). Repeat from double asterisks twice more. Pass through the next bead. Continue in peyote stitch until the cap is about ¼" (0.6 cm) long, placing it on the top of one of the cylinders occasionally to make sure it will fit. Work the last row in gold-toned size 15 beads. Pass through the last row twice to make it firm. Do not weave in ends. Make another cap for the other end of the cylinder.

Step 2 *Attaching two beadwork caps to a cylinder*

While holding one cap at each end of a cylinder, use the working thread from one of the beaded caps and string enough decorative beads to reach the other cap, having the bugle bead in the center of the decorative bead pattern (Figure 5). Pass through one bead in the last row of the end cap (Figure 6). Pass back through the strung beads and then pass through the beads in the last several rounds of the end cap to get to the other side of the end cap. String the same pattern of beads and attach it to the other side of the other end cap (Figure 7). Weave in the thread ends.

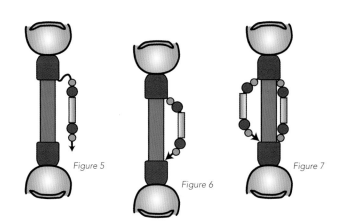

Figure 5

Figure 6

Figure 7

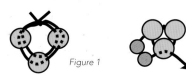

Figure 1

Figure 2

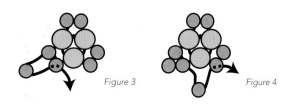

Figure 3

Figure 4

Step 3 *Adding the next cylinder while attaching the beadwork caps*

For the next cylinder, hold one cap at each end of the cylinder and, using the working thread from one of the beaded caps, string the same pattern of beads as in step 2, up to the bugle bead. Then pass through the bugle bead, string the same beads as on the first side of the bugle bead and pass through the edge beads on the beaded cap at the other end of the cylinder (Figure 8). Pass through beads in the last several rounds of the end cap to get to the other side of the end cap, string the same pattern of beads and attach it to the other side of the other end cap (Figure 9). Weave in the thread ends. Repeat this step for the remaining cylinders.

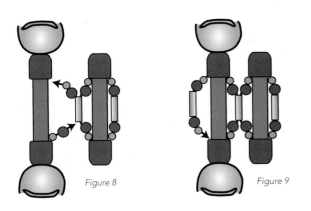

Figure 8   Figure 9

Stringing the Bracelet

Tie a 24" (61 cm) length of beading thread to the center ring on one end of the clasp with a square knot, leaving 8" (20 cm) to weave in later. String the same pattern of beads as in the photo, or add or subtract beads so that the measurement from the center of the stone section to the clasp is half the size you want the finished bracelet to be. Repeat the same pattern for all three loops on the clasps, passing through the center and outer holes of the five-hole spacer. Add the detail beads to the remaining holes on the five-hole spacers (Figure 10). Weave in ends.

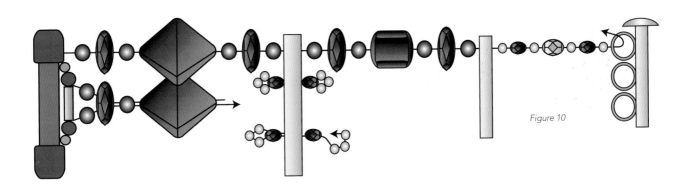

Figure 10

You can use any object for the main beadwork section, just as long as you can fit your cylinder-beaded ladder stitch section around it.

MATERIALS

Soapstone carving approx. 1⅕" (3 cm) long with ⅛" (0.3 cm) high straight sides
4 g brown size 6 seed beads
4 g brown size 8 cylinder beads (#322, Miyuki brand)
4 g iridescent bronze-toned size 11 seed beads
4 g brown size 11 seed beads
4 g dark blue/purple size 15 seed beads
4 g bronze-toned size 15 charlottes
6 or more blue 8 mm faceted beads with gold-toned edges
Approx.14 dark blue 4 mm Swarovski crystals
Size B beading thread
Size 12 beading needle
Clasp
Jump rings
Pliers

Embellishing the Carving

Step 1 *Ladder stitch and the netted bezel*

Using a 40" (102 cm) length of thread and the brown cylinder beads, make a ladder stitch strip that fits snugly around the carving. Close it into a circle by passing through the first and last beads and tying the working thread and tail into a square knot. Slide the ladder stitch circle onto the carving. *String one size 15 bead, one bronze size 11 bead, one size 15 bead and pass through the next brown cylinder bead (Figure 1). Repeat on the other side of the ladder stitch beads (Figure 2). Repeat from asterisk around twice, so that there are three beads sitting between each cylinder bead on the top and the bottom of the ladder stitch circle. Pass up through the next size 15 and 11 bead. Now close the size 11 beads into a tight circle around the top of the object by adding a size 11 bead every few beads so that the top closes tightly together with no gaps of thread. You may need to string this row several times to get the right placement and number of beads to fit evenly. Repeat on the other side of the ladder stitch beads and weave in ends.

Step 2 *Netting along the sides*

Weave in a new 40" (102 cm) length of thread so that the thread is coming out of a size 15 bead. * String one size 15 bead, pass through the next two size 15 beads (Figure 3). Repeat from asterisk around. Repeat on the other side of the ladder stitch circle. **String three charlottes, pass through the size 15 bead on the previous row (Figure 4). Repeat from double asterisks around. Pass through two charlottes. ***String one charlotte, pass through a size 15 seed bead on the other side of the carving, string one charlotte, pass through the center charlotte of the next three-bead group (Figure 5).

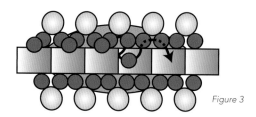

Figure 3

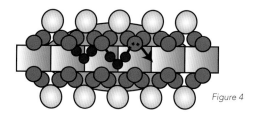

Figure 4

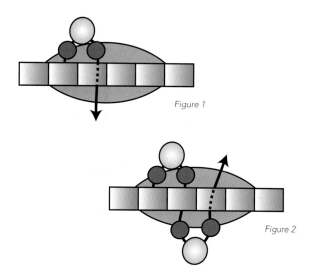

Figure 1

Figure 2

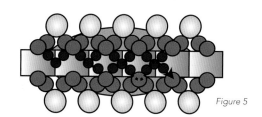

Figure 5

Stringing the Bracelet

Thread the needle with a 30" (76 cm) length of thread and pass through one of the cylinder beads approximately ¼" (0.6 cm) away from one point of the beaded carving. Remove the needle and pull the thread ends so the bead is in the middle of the thread. Thread the needle with both ends so you have a double-threaded needle. String a brown size 11 seed bead at the beginning and between each bead or bead set as follows: one crystal, one large faceted bead, one crystal, one brown size 6/cylinder three-bead set, one cylinder, one crystal, one large faceted bead, one crystal. String one brown size 11 seed bead, pass through a jump ring and all the other beads back to the carving. Weave in the end. Begin a new thread in the same way, ¼" (0.6 cm) away from the center end of the carving in the other direction. String the same bead pattern through the three-bead set, then pass through the remaining beads and jump ring. Pass back through the beads to the carving and weave in the ends. Repeat on the other side of the carving for the other half of the bracelet. Using the pliers attach several jump rings to one end and the clasp. On the other end either attach enough jump rings for the size of the bracelet you want, or string several beads between the jump ring at the end of the bracelet and a new group of jump rings to lengthen the bracelet.

celtic knot bracelet

This simple peyote stitch banded bracelet is enhanced by the twisted rope pattern, the beaded cabochon and the wonderful magnetic clasp.

MATERIALS

Round black-onyx cabochon, 13 mm diameter
2 g matte copper-colored size 11 seed beads
4 g each of cylinder beads in the following colors:
    matte black #310 (Miyuki brand)
    metallic copper #461 (Miyuki brand)
    metallic bronze #22 (Miyuki brand)
    matte copper rose #340 (Miyuki brand)
    matte brick rose #703 (Toho brand)
Backing material, ¾" x ¾"(19 mm x 19 mm) square
Size B beading thread
Size 12 beading needle
Copper-colored clasp with two holes for attachment, approx. ¼" (0.6 cm) apart
Black permanent fine point marker
Thick white glue

celtic knot bracelet

Beading Around the Cabochon

Step 1 *The base row in running stitch*

Using a small amount of glue, glue your cab to the center of the backing material. Let dry. Thread a 40" (102 cm) length of thread with the beading needle and tie a knot near the tail. Come up from the back of the backing material close to the cab. *Using the size 11 seed beads string one bead and enter the backing material about a bead's width away, next to the cab. Pass back up through the backing material one bead's width away (Figure 1). Repeat from asterisk around the cab.

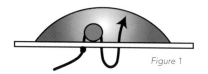

Figure 1

Step 2 *Row 2*

Pass through the first bead strung. **String one bead, pass through the next bead of the previous row (Figure 2). Repeat from double asterisks around.

Figure 2

Step 3 *Remaining rows*

Pass through the next bead (Figure 3). Repeat from the double asterisk in row 2 for each row, working one or more row of large beds and three rows of size 15 seed beads. Pass through the last row several times to tighten the beads snugly around the cab. Pass the thread down through the backing material. Do not weave in the end. Set aside.

Figure 3

Step 4 *Making the peyote stitch band and clasp attachment*

Begin the peyote stitch pattern (Figure 4), repeating the pattern from left to right and beginning with a 20" (51 cm) tail which will be used to attach the clasp later. Following the peyote stitch pattern, repeat the pattern 13 times, or until it is the desired length, including the clasp and four more rows of peyote stitch. End with a short row. Weave through the last several rows to strengthen the ends, adding a bead and passing through the clasp holes as you weave through the end beads (Figure 5). Repeat at the other end of the clasp, adding a short row as you weave through the beads. Weave in the ends.

Using the working thread from the beaded cab, stitch on the beaded cab to the center of the peyote stitch band by passing through a bead on the band, then passing through a bead on the edge of the beaded cab. Repeat around. Fill in the gaps between the first row of size 11 beads on the cab by stringing two size 15 beads then passing through a size 11 bead. Repeat around. On the back side of the bracelet, color in any backing material that shows with the permanent marker.

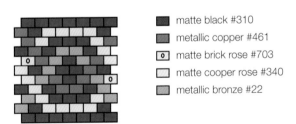

■ matte black #310
■ metallic copper #461
☐ matte brick rose #703
☐ matte cooper rose #340
■ metallic bronze #22

Figure 4

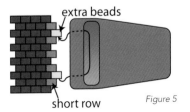

extra beads

short row   *Figure 5*

A fun discovery of how to hold a square shape in place led to this design, the basics of which are also used for the elastic-banded button bracelet on page 70.

MATERIALS

Square abalone, 16 mm x 16 mm by 3 mm thick
16 turquoise size 2 twisted bugle beads
4 g iridescent size 11 seed beads
12 silver spacer beads
8 turquoise 3 mm pearls
2 turquoise 13 mm faceted pearls
2 grey/blue 6 mm round faceted pearls
4 iridescent tapered 5 mm x 7 mm faceted drop beads
Size B beading thread
Size 12 beading needle
Toggle clasp

bugle bead abalone bracelet

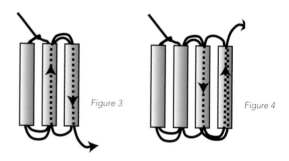

Figure 3

Figure 4

Step 2 *Adding the remaining sections*

Continuing with the thread in step 1, string three size 11 seed beads and two bugle beads. Pass through the bugle beads as shown in (Figure 2) in step 1. Make another ladder-stitch bugle-bead section as in step 1. Repeat two more times. You will have four bugle-bead sections connected by the three size 11 seed beads. String three beads and join into a circle (Figure 5). Tie the tail and working thread into a knot.

Encasing the Abalone Square

Step 1 *Beading the first ladder-stitch bugle bead section*

Using a 60" (152 cm) length of thread, string two bugle beads and tie the tail and working thread into a square knot (Figure 1), leaving a 20" (51 cm) tail to make one side of the bracelet later. Pass through both beads, string another bugle bead (Figure 2), pass through the second and third bugle beads (Figure 3). String a fourth bugle bead, pass through the third and fourth bugle beads (Figure 4). Do not weave in ends.

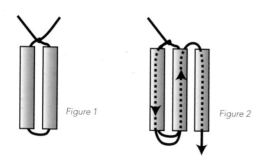

Figure 1

Figure 2

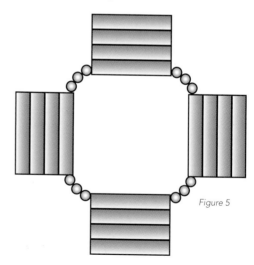

Figure 5

Step 3 *Closing around the abalone*

Pass through the bugle beads in the first section to the first bugle bead, *string three size 11 seed beads and pass through the end bugle bead in the next section (Figure 6). Repeat from asterisk until you've joined all the sections, sliding the abalone in place before stringing the last three size 11 seed beads. Pass through the beads again tightening them snugly around the abalone square. Do not weave in ends.

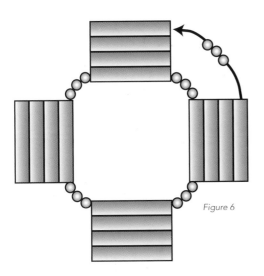

Figure 6

Stringing the Bracelet

Continuing with the working thread, pass through the bugle beads so that the thread is coming out of the second bugle bead. String five size 11 seed beads, one pearl, one spacer, one drop bead, one spacer, one round faceted pearl, one spacer, one drop bead, one spacer, one pearl, three size 11 seed beads, one pearl, one spacer, one large faceted pearl, one spacer, one pearl, 10 size 11 seed beads. Pass through the toggle section of the clasp, and back through all the beads except the first five size 11 seed beads. String five size 11 seed beads and pass through the second bugle bead on the next section of bugle beads. Pass back down the third bugle bead, string five size 11 seed beads and pass back down all the beads in the bracelet, through the toggle loop and back through all the beads except the three groups of five size 11 seed beads near the abalone. String five size 11 seed beads and pass through the remaining inner bugle bead. Weave in the end. Repeat the whole process for stringing the bracelet on the other side of the abalone, using the tail thread and the other end of the clasp. Add beads near the clasp to adjust the finished length of the bracelet.

buttons

The versatile button is a chameleon of the notions world. It can be a piece of jewelry, a decorative element on a quilt, or even just a button. This section covers ideas for using and making buttons in several ways and connects to the other project sections of the book. The first several projects are connected to the previous section as they make bracelets from buttons. The next few projects are for embellishing ready-made buttons with beads or for making buttons from other items. The last projects lead into the final section, which shows ideas for making brooches from buttons. These projects all show that buttons can be used creatively.

chapter three

It's fun to take a beautiful button and then fashion it into a bracelet like this pearl and button design. You can cut the shank to make the button lie flat, or keep it intact by using a backing thick enough to accommodate the depth of the shank. Once you have worked the beadwork with the backing around the button, you can use all sorts of designs for straps to create your one-of-a-kind bracelet.

MATERIALS

Cream button with the shank removed, ¾" (1.9 cm) or smaller diameter
Approx. 18 pale-green rectangular freshwater pearls drilled through the center
4 g gold-toned 6 mm pearls
4 g gold cylinder beads (#034 Delica brand)
4 g cream size 11 seed beads
4 g cream size 15 seed beads
4 g iridescent green size 15 seed beads
4 g green size 13 charlottes
4 g gold size 15 charlottes
4 g cream size 15 charlottes
Size B beading thread
Size 12 beading needle
Backing material, 1" x 1" (25 mm x 25 mm) square
Suede, 1" x 1" (25 mm x 25 mm) square
Clasp
Thick white glue

buttons into bracelets – mint and cream pearl bracelet

*Pass back up through the backing material about one size 11 bead's width away, string one size 11 bead, one green charlotte, and one size 11 bead, then pass back down through the backing material another size 11 bead's width away (Figure 2). Repeat from asterisk around the button. Work around the beads again, adding a green charlotte between the three-bead sets so there is a green charlotte between each pair of size 11 beads (Figure 3).

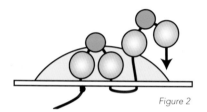

Figure 2

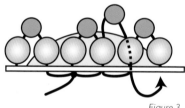

Figure 3

Encasing the Button

Step 1 *Stitching the base row and the bezel*

Using a small amount of glue, glue the button to the center of the backing material. Let dry. Thread a 40" (102 cm) length of thread with the beading needle and tie a knot near the tail. Come up from the back of the backing material close to the edge of the button. String one cream size 11 bead, one green charlotte, and one cream size 11 bead. Enter the backing material about one large bead's width away, next to the button (Figure 1).

Step 2 *Closing the bezel around the button*

Pass up through the first two beads again (Figure 4). *Working in peyote stitch, string one row using the cream size 15 seed beads, then the next row using the gold-toned size 15 charlottes, then the last row using the cream size 15 charlottes. Pass through the last row of beads several times to tighten them together so they hold the button in place. Pass back down through the backing material. Weave in the ends.

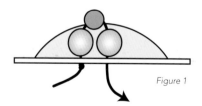

Figure 1

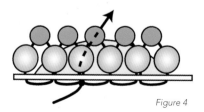

Figure 4

Stringing the Bracelet

Step 3 *Adding the pearl strap*

Attach a 40" (102 cm) length of thread to one side of the button edge. String 18 repeats of four green charlottes and one gold charlotte, omitting the last gold charlotte in the last repeat. Anchor the thread at the same place as you began on the button edge, so you have a large loop. *Pass through four green charlottes on one leg of the loop, string a pale-green freshwater pearl, skip four green charlottes on the other leg of the loop and pass through the next four green charlottes. Repeat from the asterisk until you have nine pearls. Working back toward the button, stitch through the green charlottes you skipped and pass through the pearls in the opposite direction. Weave in ends. Repeat the whole process for the other side of the button.

Step 4 *Making the spiral extension and adding the clasp*

Using a 40" (102 cm) length of thread, and leaving a 10" (25 cm) tail to attach to the clasp later, string four cream size 11 seed beads and three iridescent green size 15 seed beads. Pass back through the four cream beads, forming a circle (Figure 5). *String one

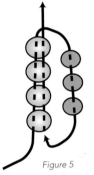

Figure 5

cream bead and three green beads (Figure 6), pass through the four cream beads closest to the needle toward the working end of the thread (Figure 7). Repeat from asterisk approx. 12 times. String one gold pearl and pass through the loop of charlottes at the end of the bracelet. Weave in that end.

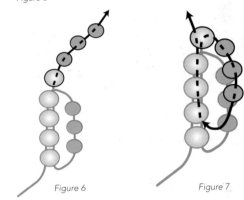

Figure 6   Figure 7

Thread the 10" (25 cm) tail, string one gold pearl and pass through one end of the clasp. Weave in that end. Repeat on the other end of the bracelet, adjusting the length of the spiral to lengthen or shorten the bracelet.

If you don't want to cut the shank off of your beautiful buttons, you can still make them into bracelets by padding the back of the button and working several extra rows of beads around your piece, as was done in this piece.

MATERIALS

Antique gold-toned oval button with a shank, 1⅛" (28 mm)
4 g matte black size 8 seed beads
4 shiny black size 8 seed beads
4 g black size 11 seed beads
4 g dark gold-toned size 11 seed beads
4 g bronze-toned size 15 charlottes
4 g antique gold-toned 3 mm bugle beads
8 black 4 mm Swarovski bicone crystals
8 antique gold-toned 4 mm faceted metal beads
2 black 6 mm cathedral beads
3-4 sheets of backing material, 1" x 2" (2.5 cm x 5 cm)
Suede, 1" x 2" (2.5 cm x 5 cm)
Size B beading thread
Size 12 beading needle
Clasp
Thick white glue
(Used for this project: La Mode button Style #26279, size 1⅛" (28 mm)

Embellishing the Button

Step 1 *Preparing the button and backing material*

Set one sheet of backing material aside. Cut a small slit in the center of the remaining sheets of backing material and fit them over the shank of the button, adding enough until the shank is hidden in the backing material. Cut them to the shape of the button and glue them together. You don't need to put glue on the button, since the shank will hold everything together. Glue the button/backing material to the center of the backing material that you set aside at the beginning. Let dry.

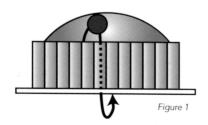

Figure 1

Step 2 *Covering the layers of backing material and making the bezel*

Using a 40" (102 cm) length of thread and the bugle beads, make a ladder-stitch strip that fits snugly around the button/backing material. Close the ladder-stitch strip into a circle by passing through the first and last beads and tying the working thread and tail into a square knot. Slide the ladder-stitch circle onto the button, sliding it down so it covers the layers of backing material. Using a running stitch, sew the circle of beads to the bottom uncut sheet of backing material, adding a shiny black size 11 bead to the top of each stitch (Figure 1). Continue in peyote stitch with the shiny black size 11 beads for a total of four rows, decreasing at the corners on the last row by passing through two beads of the previous row without adding a bead. Weave in ends.

Step 3 *Adding the suede backing and edge beadwork*

Cut the backing material close to the finished bead-work. Cut a piece of suede to the same size. Glue the suede to the backing material in the center only, using a very small amount of glue, just enough to hold it in place. Let dry. Thread a 30" (76 cm) length of thread with the beading needle and tie a knot at the tail end. Make a small stitch in the backing material to anchor the thread and hide the tail between the backing material and the suede. String one matte size 8 bead, one bronze charlotte and one matte size 8 bead. Make a small stitch through the suede and backing material and pass back through the last bead strung. *String one charlotte and one matte black size 8 bead, make a small stitch through the suede and backing material about one bead's width away and pass back through the last bead strung (Figure 2).

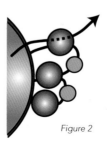

Figure 2

Repeat from asterisk around. When you get near the beginning, space your stitches so you will end up with no gaps in the beadwork. For the last stitch, pass down through the first bead that you strung. Take a small stitch in the suede and weave in the thread.

Making the Bracelet Straps

Step 4 *Stringing the charlottes*

*Thread the needle with a 20" (51 cm) length of thread and pass through one of the matte size 8 beads at one end of the beaded button. Pull the thread ends so the bead is in the middle of the thread. **String 45 bronze charlotte beads with the end that is already threaded. Pass through the last bead strung again in the direction of the thread-end to lock the beads in place. Move the needle to the other end of the thread and repeat from the double asterisks. Repeat from the single asterisk for the size 8 beads on either side of the one you've just been working out of. You will have 8 strands of charlottes at one end of the edge of the beaded button. Set aside.

Step 5 *Brick stitch triangle and braids*

*Thread the needle with a 30" (76 cm) length of thread and make a six-bead ladder-stitch strip. Work three rows of brick stitch, decreasing at each end so you form a triangle shape (Figure 3). Set aside.

Hold the charlotte strands from step 4 in sets of two and braid together. One by one, thread each thread end with a needle and pass through the brick stitch triangle on the ladder-stitch row. When all the threads are through, pull snug and adjust the braid as needed. Do not weave in the ends.

Ladder-stitch row ▶

Figure 3

Stringing the Bracelet

Thread two of the threads from the braid as one and string one shiny black size 8 seed bead, one gold size 11 bead, one metal faceted bead, one gold size 11 bead, one black crystal, one gold size 11 bead and one ¼" (0.6 cm) black faceted bead with gold ends. Repeat the sequence in reverse order, omitting the large bead. String one piece of the clasp and weave in the ends you are using. Using the other ends from the braid, pass through the brick stitch triangle so that you are exiting one of the first ladder-stitch beads at a corner. String one black size 11 bead, one gold size 11 bead, one metal faceted bead, one gold size 11 bead and one black size 11 bead. Anchor the strand at the other corner of the ladder-stitch row and weave in the ends. With a new length of thread add a similar stand of beads over the beginning of the braid. Weave in the ends. Repeat the whole process for the other side of the bracelet.

buttons into bracelets –
silver and black elastic-banded bracelet

Finished size: approx. 7½" (19 cm) to 8" (20 cm) long
Skill level: Easy

Use one button or as many as you can fit around your wrist to make this simple design that sparkles. Be sure to pull the elastic tight before tying it together so that your bracelet will keep its shape.

MATERIALS

5 or 6 silver-toned square buttons, ¾" x ¾" (19 mm x 19 mm), approx. ¹⁄₁₆" (0.2 cm) thick
Approx. 12 silver and black two-holed beads
4 g black size 11 seed beads
4 g silver-toned size 15 seed beads
4 g black large-sized cylinder beads
Approx. 24" (61 cm) .5 mm elastic line
Needle large enough to thread elastic, yet thin enough to pass through cylinder beads
Size B beading thread
Size 12 beading needle
(Used for this project: Blue Moon buttons #F6064)

Making the Button Frame
(make five or six)

Step 1 — Creating the initial circle of beads

Using a 24" (61 cm) length of beading thread, string four repeats of seven size 11 seed beads and eight size 15 seed beads. Pass through the first size 11 beads again. You now have a circle. *String eight size 15 beads, pass through the next set of size 11 beads, repeat from the asterisk twice more. Pass through the next set of size 11 beads, string eight size 15 seed beads, tie the working thread and tail into a tight square knot (Figure 1). Slide the button corners into the size 15 bead openings.

String six large cylinder beads, pass through three size 11 seed beads to the tail thread (Figure 2), tie the tail and working thread into a square knot. Weave in the ends.

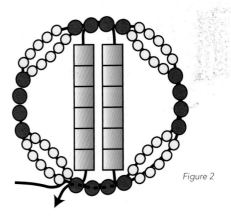

Figure 2

Stringing the Bracelet

Cut the elastic into two 12" (30 cm) pieces. Thread the larger needle with one length of elastic. Working from the back side of the buttons, **pass over the size 11 beads along the edge of the button, then through the cylinder beads, then over the size 11 beads on the other edge of the button. String one two-holed bead. Repeat from double asterisks for all the buttons, then string enough two-holed beads to make the bracelet your desired size. Repeat with the other length of elastic, passing through the remaining holes in the two-holed beads and the remaining cylinder beads.

Figure 1

Step 2 — Adding the channels for elastic thread

Pass through one size 11 bead, string six large cylinder beads, pass through two size 11 seed beads on the opposite side of the circle, as shown.

embellished bar button

Finished Size: approx. 1" (2.5 cm) long
Skill Level: Intermediate

This silver-toned button is a nice design all by itself, but I think it's often fun to embellish items to add color or give them a new look.

MATERIALS

Rectangular silver-toned button, ¾" x ⁵⁄₁₆"
   (19 mm x 8 mm)
2 silver-lined blue size 5 bugle beads
Approx. 24 pale-blue size 11 seed beads
Approx. 24 matte blue size 15 seed beads
Approx. 24 matte blue size 8 seed beads
Backing material, 1" x 1½" (25 mm x 7 mm)
Suede, approx. ½" x 1" (1.3 cm x 2.5 cm)
Size B beading thread
Size 12 beading needle
Thick white glue
Used for this project: JHB Button #1461

Step 1 *Stitching around the button*

Cut a small slit in the center of the backing material to fit over the button shank. Using a small amount of glue, glue the button to the backing material. Let dry. Thread a 40" (102 cm) length of thread with the beading needle and tie a knot near the tail. Come up from the back of the backing material alongside the button ready to string a bugle bead. *String a bugle bead and stitch it in place so that it is centered along the side of the button. Pass back up through the bugle bead and string two size 11 seed beads (Figure 1). Working in backstitch, stitch the size 11 seed beads along the short edges of the button and stitch one bugle bead along the other long edge. Pass through the beads several times to tighten the circle and hold the beads in place. End with the thread coming out of a bugle bead. String two size 15 seed beads and backstitch until you reach the remaining bugle bead. Pass through the bugle bead and stitch the size 15 seed beads again in backstitch until you reach the first bugle bead. Pass through the beads several times to tighten the circle and hold them in place. Pass through to the back of the piece. Do not weave in ends.

Figure 1

Step 2 *Finishing the edge and attaching the suede*

Cut a small slit in the center of the suede to fit over the button shank. Using a small amount of glue, glue the button to the suede, easing the shank through the hole in the suede. Let dry. Continuing with the working thread from step 1, string two size 8 beads, make a small stitch through the suede and backing material and pass back through the last bead strung. *String one bead, make a small stitch through the suede and backing material about one bead's width away and pass back through the last bead strung (Figure 2). Repeat from asterisk around. When you get near the beginning, space your stitches so you will end up with no gaps in the beadwork. For the last stitch, pass down through the first bead strung. Take a small stitch in the suede and weave in the thread.

Figure 2

Finished Size: approx. 1½" (3.8 cm) diameter
Skill Level: Intermediate

A beautiful clay button is enhanced by delicate beadwork and added coloring.

MATERIALS

Round clay button, 1" (25 mm) with a ⅛" (3 mm) flat rim
4 g green size 11 seed beads
4 g metallic burgundy size 11 seed beads
4 g red/gold-toned size 15 seed beads
4 g brown/gold size 15 seed beads
Size B beading thread
Size 12 beading needle

golden spiral button

Step 1
Making the peyote stitch band and the first row of decrease beads

Using a 40" (102 cm) length of thread and green beads, make a two-bead peyote stitch strip long enough to fit around the button. Close the strip into a circle by weaving in and out of the beginning and end and tying the working thread and tail into a square knot. Slide the bead circle onto the button. Pass through the green beads as shown, adding a burgundy size 11 bead to the top and bottom of the beaded strip (Figure 1). Repeat around a second time so there is a burgundy bead between each pair of green beads on both the top and the bottom.

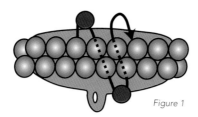

Figure 1

Step 2
Decreasing around the top of the button

Pass through one of the burgundy beads on the top of the button. *String three red/gold size 15 beads, skip the next burgundy bead, and pass through the next burgundy bead (Figure 2).

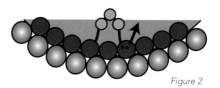

Figure 2

Repeat from asterisk around. Pass through two beads of the first three-bead set, **string two red/gold beads and pass through the second bead of the next three-bead set (Figure 3). Repeat from double asterisks around. Pass through this round several times to tighten it.

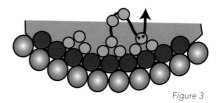

Figure 3

Pass through adjacent beads to the burgundy beads at the edge so that the thread is coming out one of the beads you skipped in the first repeat. ***String three red/gold size 15 beads, pass through the next burgundy bead skipped in the first repeat (Figure 4). Repeat from triple asterisks around. Pass the thread down to the burgundy beads on the bottom of the button.

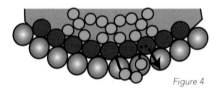

Figure 4

Step 3 *Decreasing around the bottom of the button*

Working in the burgundy beads on the bottom side of the button, stitch three rows of peyote stitch using the brown/gold size 15 seed beads. After the last row, pass through the last row of beads only, not the previous row, and pull tightly to tighten the beading around the button. Weave in ends.

A small bead by Sarah Nelson Shriver is transformed into a layer-cake-like button. With the delicate bead backs available at beading stores, you can make just about anything into a button.

MATERIALS

Approx. 75 green size 8 seed beads
50 dark gold-toned size 11 seed beads
25 green size 12 charlotte beads
Polymer clay bead, ½" (13 mm) diameter x ⅛" (3 mm) tall
Backing material, 1" x 1" (25 mm x 25 mm) square
Suede, 1" x 1" (25 mm x 25 mm) square
Metal button back
Size B beading thread
Size 12 beading needle
Thick white glue
Permanent glue

polymer clay bead into a button

Step 2 *The top two rows of beads*

Continuing with the thread from step 1, **string one green size 8 bead, pass back through the bead below on the first row (Figure 2), then through the bead just strung on the top row (Figure 3). Repeat from double asterisk for the second row. Pass through the beads several times to tighten the circle and hold the beads in place. Work another row of backstitch in the same manner, using the size 11 gold-toned beads, only stringing enough beads to make a tight circle around the top of the polymer clay bead to hold it in place. Pass through this row several times to tighten the circle and hold the polymer clay bead in place.

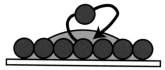

Figure 2

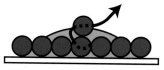

Figure 3

Step 1 *The first row around the polymer clay bead*

Thread a 40" (102 cm) length of thread with the beading needle and tie a knot near the tail. Come up from the back of the backing material and sew the polymer clay bead to the center of the backing material. To begin beading, come up from the backing material close to the edge of the polymer clay. *Using the green size 8 beads, string two beads and enter the backing material about two beads' width away, next to the polymer clay. Pass back up through the backing material between the two beads, pass through the last bead strung (Figure 1). Repeat from asterisk around the polymer clay. Pass through the beads several times to tighten the beads snugly around the cab.

Figure 1

Step 3 *Finishing the edge and attaching the suede*

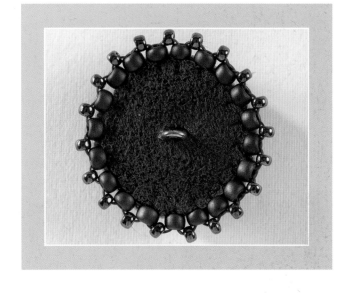

Using the permanent glue, glue the button back to the back of the piece. Let dry. Cut a small slit in the center of the suede to fit over the button shank. Using a small amount of thick white glue, glue the suede to the back of the button, easing the shank through the hole in the suede. Let dry. Continuing with the working thread from step 1, string one size 8 bead, one size 11 bead and one size 8 bead. Make a small stitch through the suede and backing material and pass back through the last bead strung. *String one size 11 bead and one size 8 bead. Then make a small stitch through the suede and backing material about one bead's width away and pass back through the last bead strung (Figure 4). Repeat from asterisk around. When you get near the beginning, space your stitches so you will end up with no gaps in the beadwork. For the last stitch, pass down through the first bead strung. String one charlotte, then pass through the beads along the edge you just added, stringing a charlotte between the size 8 beads (Figure 5). Take a small stitch in the suede and weave in the thread.

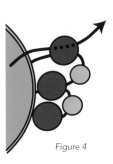

Figure 4

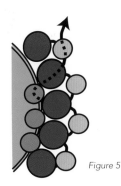

Figure 5

malachite and netting-covered button

Finished Size: approx. 1½" (3.8 cm) diameter
Skill Level: Intermediate

Covered buttons you make lend themselves to embellishment. The trick to this project is to bead your cabochon onto the fabric before forming the button. However, you will need to have the finished beaded cabochon small enough so that you can form the button without putting a lot of pressure on the cab.

MATERIALS

Round malachite cabochon, ¾" (19 mm)
Approx. 35 dark-green size 8 seed beads
4 g green size 11 seed beads
4 g blue size 15 seed beads
Dark-green fabric, 2" x 2" (5 cm x 5 cm) square
Thin fusible interfacing, 2" x 2" (5 cm x 5 cm) square
Size B beading thread
Size 12 beading needle
Covered button kit for 1" (2.5 cm) button
Thick white glue

Step 1 *Attaching the cab and stitching the base row*

Fuse the interfacing to the wrong side of the fabric, following the manufacturer's instructions. Using a small amount of glue, glue the cabochon to the right side in the center of the fabric. Let dry. Thread a 40" (102 cm) length of thread with the beading needle and tie a knot near the tail. Come up from the back of the fabric close to the cab. *Using the green size 8 beads string two beads and enter the backing material about two beads' width away, next to the cab. Pass back up through the backing material between the two beads, pass through the last bead strung (Figure 1). Repeat from asterisk around the cab. Pass through the beads several times to tighten the beads snugly around the cab. Pass down through the backing material.

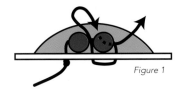

Figure 1

Step 2 *Stitching the bezel row*

Pass up through the backing material between the cab and the row of size 8 beads. *Using the blue size 15 seed beads string two beads and enter the backing material about two beads' width away, between the cab and the larger beads. Pass back up through the backing material between the two beads, pass through the last bead strung (Figure 2). Repeat from asterisk around the cab. Pass through the beads several times

to tighten the beads snugly around the cab. Pass down through the backing material, then up through one of the green size 8 seed beads. Do not weave in the end.

Step 3 *Covering the button*

Following the manufacturer's instructions, cover the button using the beaded fabric. The beadwork and the cab should fit inside the button-making tool so you are not putting pressure on the cab or beads.

Step 4 *Stitching the netting*

Continuing with the working thread, *string three green size 11 beads, skip one size 8 bead, pass through the next size 8 bead. Repeat from asterisk around. Pass through the first two beads in the row. **String five size 11 beads, pass through the middle size 11 bead of the next three-bead group. Repeat from the double asterisks around. Pass through the first three beads in the row. ***Take a backstitch in the button fabric near the button back. Pass through the bead the thread was exiting. String three beads, pass through the third bead of the next five-bead group. Repeat from the triple asterisks around. Weave in ends.

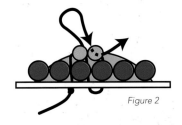

Figure 2

buttons into brooches – cream floral swirl

This button doesn't actually have any cream color when you buy it at the store. It's black in the crevices. I wanted a lighter-colored project, so I bought some acrylic paint, painted over the button, then wiped off the excess with a paper towel while the paint was wet. It took a few tries to get the right look, then Voila! I had the button I wanted. The cream paint stayed in the crevices and the gold tone on top shone through. Spray the button with a sealer and you have a new button. You can try this with different types of buttons and colors of paint to see if you can come up with just the right color or look for your piece.

MATERIALS

Round button with shank cut off, ⅞" (2.2 cm) diameter
Approx. 22 cream size 6 seed beads
4 g gold-toned size 8 seed beads
4 g cream size 15 seed beads
Approx. 22 white 6 mm pearls
Backing material, 1½" x 1½" (38 mm x 38 mm) square
Suede, 1½" x 1½" (38 mm x 38 mm) square
Size B beading thread
Size 12 beading needle
1" long pin back
Thick white glue
(Used for this project: JHB International ⅞" (22 mm) #1141 (front of card)
or 93196 (bar code number)

buttons into brooches – cream floral swirl

Step 2 *Stitching the bezel row*

Pass up through the backing material between the button and the row of size 8 beads. *Using the size 15 seed beads string two beads and enter the backing material about two beads' width away, between the button and the larger beads. Pass back up through the backing material between the two beads, pass through the last bead strung (Figure 2). Repeat from asterisk around the button. Pass through the beads several times to tighten the beads snugly around the button. Pass down through the backing material.

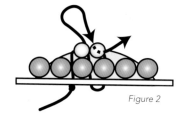

Figure 2

Step 1 *Stitching the base row*

Using a small amount of glue, attach the button to the center of the backing material. Let dry. Thread a 40" (102 cm) length of thread with the beading needle and tie a knot near the tail. Come up from the back of the backing material close to the edge of the button. *Using the gold-toned size 8 beads, string two beads and enter the backing material about two beads' width away, next to the button. Pass back up through the backing material between the two beads, pass through the last bead strung (Figure 1). Repeat from asterisk around the button. Pass through the beads several times to tighten the beads snugly around the button. Pass down through the backing material.

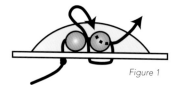

Figure 1

Step 3 *Adding the pin back and suede backing*

Cut the backing material close to the finished beadwork. Using the permanent glue, attach the pin back to the upper center of the back of the button. Let dry. Position the suede over the back of the button and lightly mark where the ends of the pin are located. Cut a small slit at each marking on the suede and slide onto the pin back. Glue the suede to the backing material in the center only, using a very small amount of thick white glue, just enough to hold it in place. Let dry. Trim the suede to the same size as the backing material. Thread a 40" (102 cm) length of thread with the beading needle and tie a knot at the tail end. Make a small stitch in the backing material to anchor the thread and hide the tail between the backing material and the suede. String one cream size 6 bead, one cream size 15 bead and one cream size 6 bead. Make a small stitch through the suede and backing material and pass back through the last bead strung. *String one size 15 bead, one size 6 bead, and make a small stitch through the suede about one size 6 bead's width away and pass back through the last bead strung (Figure 3).

Repeat from asterisk around. When you get near the beginning, space your stitches so you will end up with no gaps in the beadwork. For the last stitch, pass down through the first bead strung. Take a small stitch in the suede and pass back up through a size 6 bead. **String one pearl, three size 15 beads and pass back down through the pearl, the size 6 bead and back up through the next size 6 bead (Figure 4). Repeat from the double asterisks around. Weave in ends.

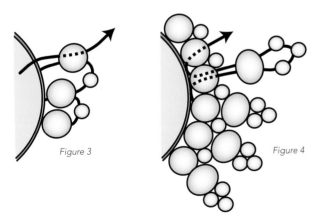

Figure 3   Figure 4

Susan Clarke Originals has a wonderful option for its clay buttons. You can ask to have them with or without a shank. This design has no shank so it was perfect for using as a cabochon in a brooch setting.

MATERIALS

Clay button with no shank, 1¼" (32 mm)
4 g blue size 8 seed beads
4 g light-blue size 11 seed beads
2 g blue size 11 seed beads
2 g white size 18 seed beads
Backing material, 2" x 2" (5 cm x 5 cm) square
Suede, 2" x 2" (5 cm x 5 cm) square
Size B beading thread
Size 12 beading needle
Pin back
Thick white glue
Permanent glue
Used for this project: Susan Clarke Originals #1049-N

buttons into brooches – blue and white clay

Step 2 *Stitching the bezel row*

Pass up through the backing material between the button edge and the row of size 8 beads. *Using the light-blue size 11 seed beads, string two beads and enter the backing material about two beads' width away, between the button edge and the size 8 beads. Pass back up through the backing material between the two beads, pass through the last bead strung (Figure 2). Repeat from asterisk around the button. Pass through the beads several times to tighten the beads snugly in place. Pass down through the backing material. Weave in the end.

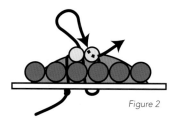

Figure 2

Step 1 *Stitching the base row*

Using a small amount of thick white glue, glue your button to the center of the backing material. Let dry. Thread a 40" (102 cm) length of thread with the beading needle and tie a knot near the tail. Come up from the back of the backing material close to the button edge. *Using the size 8 beads, string two beads and enter the backing material about two beads' width away, next to the cab. Pass back up through the backing material between the two beads, pass through the last bead strung (Figure 1). Repeat from asterisk around the button. Pass through the beads several times to tighten the beads snugly in place. Pass down through the backing material.

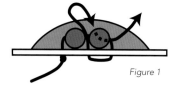

Figure 1

Step 3 *Adding the suede backing*

Cut the backing material close to the finished bead-work. Using the permanent glue, adhere the pin back to the upper center back of the piece. Place the suede over the back and lightly mark the suede at the two ends of the pin back. Cut a small slit at each marking and slide the suede into place. Pull the suede up enough to glue it into place in the center only, using a very small amount of thick white glue. Let dry. Cut the suede to match the back of the piece. Thread a 40" (102 cm) length of thread with the beading needle and tie a knot at the tail end. Make a small stitch in the backing material to anchor the thread and hide the tail between the backing material and the suede. String two light-blue size 11 seed beads, make a small stitch through the suede and backing material and pass back through the last bead strung. *String one light-blue size 11 seed bead, make a small stitch through the suede about one bead's width away and pass back through the last bead strung (Figure 3). Repeat from asterisk around. When you get near the beginning, space your stitches so you will end up with no gaps in the beadwork. For the last stitch, pass down through the first bead strung. Take a small stitch in the suede and pass out through the next bead. Do not weave in the end.

Figure 3

Step 4 *Adding the detail edging*

Work one row of brick stitch, alternating a light-blue size 11 seed bead with a blue size 11 seed bead. Work another row of brick stitch, using the blue size 8 seed beads, adding a light-blue size 11 seed bead between each stitch. Pass through the beads to the first back stitch row from step 1. Work backstitches in every third bead, adding five small white beads to the backstitches. Weave in ends.

brooches

Brooches, or decorative pins and clasps, are some of the most versatile pieces of jewelry you can make. Almost anything can become a brooch, from a favorite button to a photo or a special shell picked up on a beach. Brooches can be precious little works of art or mementos of special moments in your life. Here are just a few of the ways you can make brooches — from simply beading around a cabochon to making a composition with several cabochons or making a layered project with a hinged opening.

chapter four

Small pins or lapel brooches are quick, easy, and fun to make accessories which make great gifts, and you can coordinate the colors to match your blouse or jacket. The following instructions are for the rose and purple stick pin. The blue stick pin is made in the same manner using different beads.

MATERIALS

One ½" button
Purple ¼" nail head
Approx. 15 burgundy 4 mm fire-polished beads
Approx. 30 purple size 15 seed beads
Approx. 25 pink size 11 seed beads
Approx. 15 purple size 8 triangle beads
Backing material, 1" x 1" (2.5 cm x 2.5 cm) square
Suede, 1" x 1" (2.5 cm x 2.5 cm) square
Size B beading thread
Size 12 beading needle
Stick pin
Thick white glue
Permanent jewelry adhesive

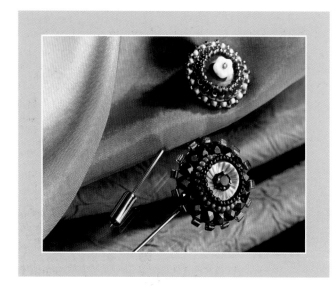

Beading Around the Cabochon

Step 1 *Stitching the base row*

Using the beading needle and thread, sew the button and nail head bead to the center of the backing material, by tying a knot near the tail end of the thread, passing up through the backing material, the back of the button, and the nail head, then passing back down through the button and the backing material. Repeat several times so the button and nail head are securely attached to the backing material. Thread a 40" (102 cm) length of thread with the beading needle and tie a knot near the tail. Come up from the back of the backing material close to the cab. *Using the size 11 beads, string two beads and enter the backing material about two beads' width away, next to the cab. Pass back up

through the backing material between the two beads, pass through the last bead strung (Figure 1). Repeat from asterisk around the cab. Pass through the beads several times to tighten the beads snugly around the cab. Pass down through the backing material.

Step 2 *Stitching the bezel row*

Pass up through the backing material between the cab and the row of size 11 beads. *Using the size 15 beads string two beads and enter the backing material about two bead's width away, between the cab and the size 11 beads. Pass back up through the backing material between the two beads, pass through the last bead strung (Figure 2). Repeat from asterisk around the cab. Pass through the beads several times to tighten the beads snugly around the cab. Pass down through the backing material.

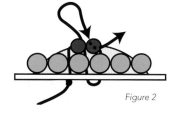

Figure 2

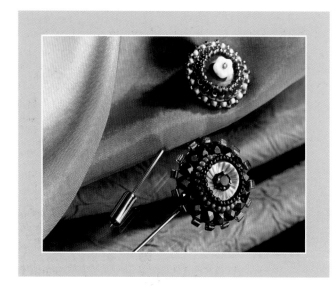

Figure 1

Step 3 *Attaching the pin back and suede backing*

Cut the backing material close to the finished beadwork. Using the permanent glue, glue the stick pin to the center of the back of the beaded button. Let dry. Center the suede over the back of the button and pierce it with the glued stick pin, sliding it in to place over the button. Lift the suede slightly, and glue the center section over the stick pin with a thin layer of thick white glue. Trim the suede so it is the same size as the button. Thread a 24" (61 cm) length of thread with the beading needle and tie a knot at the tail end. Make a small stitch in the backing material to anchor the thread and hide the tail between the backing material and the suede. String one fire-polished bead, one triangle bead, one fire-polished bead. Make a small stitch through the suede and backing material and pass back through the last bead strung. *String one triangle bead, one fire-polished bead. Make a small stitch through the suede and backing material, about one bead's width away and pass back through the last bead strung (Figure 3). Repeat from asterisk around. When you get near the beginning, space your stitches so you will end up with no gaps in the beadwork. For the last stitch, pass down through the first bead strung. Weave in ends.

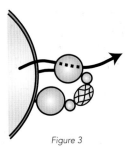

Figure 3

This asymmetrical design has an interesting feature: it uses a shawl stick pin to hold it in place. This makes it the perfect accessory to hold your favorite scarf or shawl in place.

MATERIALS

Asymmetrical green cabochon, 1¾" x 1¼" (44 mm x 32 mm) or approx. size
4 g green size 6 seed beads
4 g cream size 8 seed beads
4 g gold-toned size 11 seed beads
4 g cream size 11 seed beads
14 g green size 11 seed beads
Approx. 25 green 3 mm-long fire-polished beads
Backing material, 1½" by 2¼" (3.8 cm x 5.7 cm)
Suede, 1½" by 2¼" (3.8 cm x 5.7 cm)
Size B beading thread
Size 12 beading needle
Thick white glue
Used for this project: Gita Maria Knit Stick KY410AE01

fringed brooch

Step 1 _Stitching the base row_

Using a small amount of glue, glue your cabochon to the center of the backing material. Let dry. Thread a 40" (102 cm) length of thread with the beading needle and tie a knot near the tail. Come up from the back of the backing material close to the cab. *Using the green size 6 beads, string two beads and enter the backing material about two beads' width away, next to the cab. Pass back up through the backing material between the two beads, pass through the last bead strung (Figure 1). Repeat from asterisk around the cab. Pass through the beads several times to tighten the beads snugly around the cab. Pass down through the backing material.

Figure 1

Step 2 _Stitching the bezel row_

Pass up through the backing material between the cab and the row of size 6 beads. *Using the size 11 seed beads string one green and one cream bead and enter the backing material about two beads' width away, between the cab and the size 6 beads. Pass back up through the backing material between the two beads, pass through the last bead strung (Figure 2). Repeat from asterisk around the cab. Pass through the beads several times to tighten the beads snugly around the cab. Pass down through the backing material.

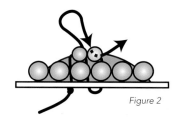

Figure 2

Step 3 _Attaching the pin back and suede backing_

Cut the backing material close to the finished beadwork. Trim the suede so it is the same size as the cab and glue in place using a small amount of thick white glue. Thread a 40" (102 cm) length of thread with the beading needle and tie a knot at the tail end. Make a small stitch in the backing material to anchor the thread and hide the tail between the backing material and the suede. String two cream size 8 seed beads. Make a small stitch through the suede and backing material and pass back through the last bead strung. *String one cream size 8 seed bead and make a small stitch through the suede and backing material about one bead's width away and pass back through the last bead strung (Figure 3). Repeat from asterisk around. When you get near the beginning, space your stitches so you will end up with no gaps in the beadwork. For the last stitch, pass down through the first bead strung. Take a small stitch in the suede, then pass back up through the same bead.

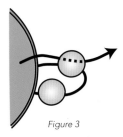

Figure 3

To fill the gap between the cream size 11 beads and the green size 6 beads, **pass down through the next cream bead, string one gold size 11 bead, pass up through the next cream bead. Repeat from double asterisks around. Pass through the gold beads again, stringing another gold bead between each bead. Weave in the ends.

Step 4 The fringe

Attach a new length of thread at one of the corners of the piece so the thread is coming out of a cream size 8 seed bead. String 10 green size 11 seed beads, one cream size 11 seed bead, one gold size 11 seed bead, one green fire-polished bead, and three gold size 11 seed beads. Skip the last three beads and pass back up through all the other beads and through the cream size 8 seed bead on the edge of the cab. Pass

back down through the next cream size 8 seed bead and string the same sequence of beads for the next dangle, except string two more green size 11 seed beads than the previous dangle. Repeat the process for each dangle to the lowest point of the cab. Then work several dangles with the same number of green size 11 seed beads, and then begin using two fewer beads for each dangle until you reach the next corner of the cab. Weave in ends.

Step 5 Loops for the stick pin

Attach a new length of the thread on the back of the cab, near the side. String eight green size 11 seed beads and make a small loop along the cream size 8 bead edging. Stitch several times through the loop to make a strong structure. Repeat on the other side of the cab. Weave in ends. Use these loops and your stick pin to hold the brooch on your scarf.

You can make a brooch similar to this one, although yours will be unique to your beads, cabochons and personal taste. Work from the center out, planning and changing your design as your beading progresses. You may be surprised to see that your piece takes on its own look as you adjust the pattern to fit your beading style.

MATERIALS

Central jade cabochon, ½" x ¾" (13 mm x 19 mm) or approx. size
2 small lapis lazuli 4 mm x 6 mm oval cabochons (or approx. size)
2 lapis lazuli 8 mm x 13 mm triangle-shaped cabochons (or approx. size)
Approx. 24 blue size 8 seed beads
24 gold-toned size 8 seed beads
6 g iridescent blue/purple size 8 seed beads
4 g iridescent blue/purple size 11 seed beads
4 g green size 15 seed beads
4 g iridescent blue/brown size 15 seed beads
2 g bronze size 15 charlottes
2 g purple size 15 charlottes
4 g green size 2 bugle beads
Backing material, 2½" x 3½" (6.4 cm x 8.9 cm)
Suede, 2½" x 3½" (6.4 cm x 8.9 cm)
Cardboard or sheet metal, 2½" x 3½" (6.4 cm x 8.9 cm)
Size B beading thread
Size 12 beading needle
Pin back
Thick white glue
Permanent glue
Ruler

stone collection brooch

Step 1 *Preparing the backing*

Draw a pencil line across the center of the backing material horizontally and vertically so you know where the center is and you have lines to the sides, top and bottom (Figure 1). You will need these to keep your stones even.

Step 2 *Beading the central stone in place*

Using the thick white glue, glue the large oval stone to the center of the backing material. Let dry. Bead the stone in place using the backstitch bezel setting method (page 22) with the blue size 8 seed beads for the base row and the green size 15 seed beads for the bezel row. Bead a third row of backstitch around the base row alternating the gold-toned size 8 beads with the blue/purple size 8 beads (Figure 2).

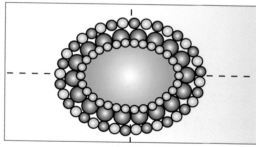

Figure 2

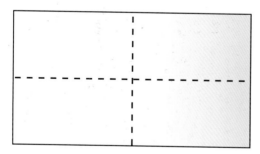

Figure 1

Step 3 *Adding the surrounding stones*

Using the thick white glue, glue the small oval stone above and below the center stone leaving enough space for two bead rows between the small stones and the center stone. Bead the stones in place using the backstitch bezel setting method (page 22) with the blue/purple size 11 beads for the base row and the green size 15 beads for the bezel row. Repeat the process for the triangle-shaped stones, using the same method and beads to stitch them in place (Figure 3).

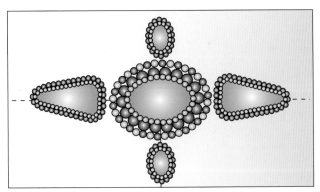

Figure 3

Step 4 *Beading the remaining surface*

Backstitch two rows of purple size 15 charlottes around the large central cab, changing to one row if needed between the large stone and the smaller stones. Using single stitches, sew the bugle beads, radiating out from the purple rows of beads. Backstitch a row of bronze size 15 charlottes around the perimeter of the design, then another row of blue/purple size 8 beads.

Step 5 *Finishing*

Trim the backing material close to the beadwork. Draw the outline of the beadwork shape onto the cardboard or metal sheeting and cut it out just inside the line, so the piece is a little smaller than the finished beading. Glue the beadwork to the cardboard or metal with the permanent glue. Glue the pin back to the upper center of the back of the beadwork with the permanent glue. Let dry. Place the suede on the back of the beadwork and mark where the two ends of the pin back are, then cut small slits at the markings and slide the suede onto the pin back. Using the thick white glue, attach the suede in place, leaving the edges unglued. Trim the suede to the same size as the finished beadwork. Using the classic bead edging finish the edge using blue/purple size 11 seed beads and blue/brown size 15 seed beads.

Finished Size: approx. 2" (5 cm) diameter, not including fringe
Skill Level: Intermediate

A stone flower with flowers hanging in the fringe are the elements of this design. The peyote stitch border around the main stone has an organic feel since the stone shape is not uniform, so I added more beads randomly to finished rows and decreased randomly from size 11 beads to size 15.

MATERIALS

Carved salmon-colored 38 mm flower-shaped cabochon
Approx. 7 g cream size 11 seed beads
4 g pale-green size 15 seed beads
4 g cream size 3 bugle beads
4 salmon-colored 3 mm fire-polished beads
Approx. 20 pale-green 6 mm flower spacer beads
Approx. 20 tear-shaped salmon-colored 9 mm x 11 mm side-drilled faceted drop beads
5 carved 25 mm flower beads (two wide and three narrow, or any you can find)
Backing material, 2" x 2" (5 cm x 5 cm) square
Suede, 2" x 2" (5 cm x 5 cm) square
Size B beading thread
Size 12 beading needle
Thick white glue
Permanent glue
Pin back

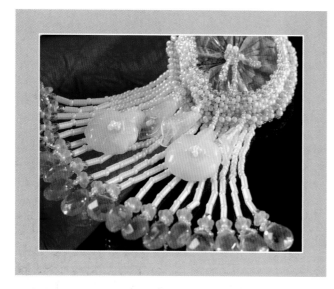

Step 1 *The base row in running stitch*

Using a small amount of glue, glue your cabochon to the center of the backing material. Let dry. Thread a 40" (102 cm) length of thread with the beading needle and tie a knot near the tail. Come up from the back of the backing material close to the cab. *Using the cream size 11 seed beads string one bead and enter the backing material about a bead's width away, next to the cab. Pass back up through the backing material one bead's width away (Figure 1). Repeat from asterisk around the cab.

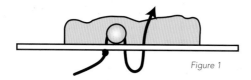

Figure 1

Step 2 *Row 2*

Pass through the first bead strung. **String one bead, pass through the next bead of the previous row (Figure 2). Repeat from double asterisks around.

Figure 2

Step 3 *Remaining rows and center decoration*

Pass through the next bead. Repeat from the double asterisk in row 2 for each row, changing to the green size 15 seed beads after a few rows to close the beads around the cab. Pass through the last row several times to tighten the beads snugly around the cab. Weave in the ends.

If your stone has a hole in the middle, attach a 30" length of thread to the center of the backing material and string three or more dangles on the front side of the piece. Weave in the ends.

Step 4 *Adding the suede backing*

Cut the backing material close to the finished beadwork. Using the permanent glue, attach the pin back to the upper center back of the beadwork. Let dry. Place the suede over the back of the beadwork and mark the ends of the pin back. Cut a small slit at the marking and slide the suede over the pin back. Glue the suede to the backing material in the center only, using a very small amount of glue, just enough to hold it in place. Let dry. Trim the suede to the size of the beadwork. Thread a 24" (61 cm) length of thread with the beading needle and tie a knot at the tail end. Make a small stitch in the backing material to anchor the thread and hide the tail between the backing material and the suede. String two cream size 11 seed beads, make a small stitch through the suede and backing material and pass back through the last bead strung. *String one bead, make a small stitch through the suede and backing material about one bead's width away and pass back through the last bead strung (Figure 3). Repeat from asterisk around. When you get near the beginning, space your stitches so you will end up with no gaps in the beadwork. For the last stitch, pass down through the first bead strung. Take a small stitch in the suede and weave in the thread.

Step 5 *Making the fringe*

Attach a new 60" (152 cm) length of thread to the bottom center edge of the beadwork, pulling the thread through so you can use half for the fringe in one direction and half in the other direction. *String 20 cream size 11 beads, one bugle, one cream size 11, one bugle, one cream size 11, one bugle, one salmon fire-polished bead, one green flower spacer, one cream size 11, three green size 15 seed beads, one faceted drop bead, and three size 15 green seed beads. Skip the last seven beads and pass back up through all the other beads and through the cream bead along the edge of the beaded stone. Pass back down through the next cream bead along the stone's edge and repeat from the asterisk for each dangle for about 1" (2.5 cm) along the bottom edge of the beaded stone. Repeat for the other side of the center dangle using the other end of the thread. Weave in the ends.

Figure 3

leaf & stone brooch

This classic backstitch beaded pin is enhanced with an interesting carved leaf dangling below the pin.

MATERIALS

Triangular or oval-shaped cabochon, 13 mm
Carved stone leaf with a side-drilled hole in the stem, approx. 38 mm
4 g matte brown size 6 seed beads
4 g matte black size 8 seed beads
4 g gold-toned size 11 seed beads
Backing material, 2" x 2" (5 cm x 5 cm) square
Suede, 2" x 2" (5 cm x 5 cm) square
Size B beading thread
Size 11 beading needle
Thick white glue
Permanent glue
Pin back

leaf & stone brooch

Step 2 *Stitching the bezel row*

Pass up through the backing material between the cab and the row of black size 8 beads. *Using the gold-toned size 11 seed beads, string two beads. Enter the backing material about two beads' width away, between the cab and the black size 8 beads. Pass back up through the backing material between the two beads, pass through the last bead strung (Figure 2). Repeat from asterisk around the cab. Pass through the beads several times to tighten the beads snugly around the cab. Pass down through the backing material.

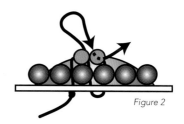

Figure 2

Step 1 *Stitching the base row*

Using a small amount of glue, glue your cabochon to the center of the backing material. Let dry. Thread a 40" (102 cm) length of thread with the beading needle and tie a knot near the tail. Come up from the back of the backing material close to the cab. *Using the black size 8 beads, string two beads and enter the backing material about two beads' width away, next to the cab. Pass back up through the backing material between the two beads, pass through the last bead strung (Figure 1). Repeat from asterisk around the cab. Pass through the beads several times to tighten the beads snugly around the cab. Pass down through the backing material.

Figure 1

Step 3 *Adding the suede backing*

Cut the backing material close to the finished beadwork. Using the permanent glue, adhere the pin back to the upper center back of the piece. Place the suede over the back and lightly mark the suede at the two ends of the pin back. Cut a small slit at each marking and slide the suede in place. Pull the suede up enough to glue it in place in the center only, using a very small amount of glue. Let dry. Cut the suede to match the back of the piece. Thread a 40" (102 cm) length of thread with the beading needle and tie a knot at the tail end. Make a small stitch in the backing material to anchor the thread and hide the tail between the backing material and the suede. String one brown size 6 seed bead, one gold-toned size 11 seed bead and one brown size 6 seed bead. Make a small stitch through the suede and backing material and pass back through the last bead strung. *String one gold-toned size 11 seed bead and one brown size 6 seed bead, make a small stitch through the suede about one bead's width away and pass back through the last bead strung (Figure 3). Repeat from asterisk around. When you get near the beginning, space your stitches so you will end up with no gaps in the beadwork. For the last stitch, pass down through the first bead strung. Take a small stitch in the suede and pass out through the next bead. Do not weave in the end.

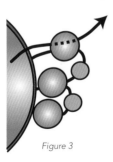

Figure 3

Step 4 *The Leaf*

Pass the working thread through the edge beads until you are coming out of one of the four brown size 6 seed beads near the bottom of the edge of the piece. String one black size 8 seed bead, one brown size 6 seed bead, one black size 8 seed bead, five gold-toned size 11 seed beads, the stone leaf, five gold-toned size 11 seed beads, one black size 8 seed bead, one brown size 6 seed bead, and one black size 8 seed bead. Pass up through the last bead of the four-bead grouping at the bottom of the piece and weave over to the beginning and pass through the beads again. Weave through to the gold-toned size 11 seed bead at the middle bottom of the piece, string three beads and pass through the bead again. Weave in the ends.

free-form brooch

Here is where you can just bead and bead and let the beads take you where they want to go. Your only restriction is the finished size and shape of your piece, but other than that you can have fun trying out techniques and color combinations. It's a great way to save a special memory, such as a small shell or stone from a wonderful vacation, or a good way to use leftovers from other projects so you have room in your bead box to ... buy more beads of course!

MATERIALS

Several large and small cabochons ranging from a little over 6 mm to 25 mm in diameter

An assortment of beads in a range of colors to go with the cabochons, sizes 15 to 8

Unusual bead shapes or charms to bead around

Backing material, 2½" x 3½" (6.4 cm x 8.9 cm)

Suede, 2½" x 3½" (6.4 cm x 8.9 cm)

Oval wood shape, 3¼" by 1¼" (8.3 cm x 3.2 cm)

Size B beading thread

Size 12 beading needle

Pin back

Thick white glue

Permanent glue

Steps

There aren't too many instructions for this piece because you will be the designer. I suggest browsing through the technique section on pages 18–27 and trying out something you haven't done before or combining different ideas. Begin by choosing where you want your stones. Glue and bead them in place, then experiment with different beading techniques and colors. Have fun. Finish the back the same as the other brooches in this section.

It's a challenge to get a photo small enough to fit under a glass cabochon, but once you do, you'll have fun seeing the faces watching you as you bead.

MATERIALS

Oblong cabochon, approx. 44 mm long by 13 mm tall with a transparent section
6 g green size 11 seed beads
3 g pale-blue size 15 seed beads
Approx. 5 pale-green 4 mm x 6 mm oval beads
4 blue 3 mm drop beads
2 green tapered 6 mm x 7 mm faceted beads
1 pale-blue 5 mm x 8 mm faceted drop bead
Backing material, 2½" x 1" (6.4 cm x 2.5 cm)
Suede, 2½" x 1" (6.4 cm x 2.5 cm)
Optional: ½" (1.3 cm) tall photo
Size B beading thread
Size 12 beading needle
Pin back
Thick white glue
Permanent glue

Step 2 *Row 2*

Pass through the first bead strung. **String one bead, pass through the next bead of the previous row (Figure 2). Repeat from double asterisks around.

Figure 2

Step 1 *The base row in running stitch*

Center your glass cabochon on the backing material and outline the shape lightly with a pencil. Using a small amount of glue, glue the photo to the backing material where you want it to show through the cab. Let dry. Thread a 40" (102 cm) length of thread with the beading needle and tie a knot near the tail. Come up from the back of the backing material on the line you drew around the cab. *Using the green size 11 seed beads string one bead and enter the backing material about a bead's width away on the pencil line. Pass back up through the backing material one bead's width away (Figure 1). Repeat from asterisk around the pencil line.

Step 3 *Remaining rows*

Pass through the next bead. Set the cab in place and hold it there as you bead until the beadwork can keep it in place. Repeat from the double asterisk in step 2 for each row, changing to the pale-blue size 15 seed beads for the last row to close the beads around the cab. Use one bead around the corners and alternate two beads then one bead, or any combination that fills the spaces, yet closes the beadwork around the cab. Pass through the last row several times to tighten the beads snugly around the cab. Weave in the ends.

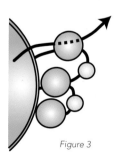

Figure 3

Figure 1

Step 4 *Adding the suede backing*

Cut the backing material close to the finished beadwork. Using the permanent glue, attach the pin back to the upper center back of the beadwork. Let dry. Place the suede over the back of the beadwork and mark the ends of the pin back. Cut a small slit at the marking and slide the suede over the pin back. Glue the suede to the backing material in the center only, using a very small amount of glue, just enough to hold it in place. Let dry. Trim the suede to the size of the beadwork. Thread a 24" (61 cm) length of thread with the beading needle and tie a knot at the tail end. Make a small stitch in the backing material to anchor the thread and hide the tail between the backing material and the suede. *String one green size 11 bead, one pale-blue size 15 bead and one green size 11 bead. Make a small stitch through the suede about one bead's width away and pass back through the last bead strung (Figure 3). Repeat from asterisk around. When you get near the beginning, space your stitches so you will end up with no gaps in the beadwork. For the last stitch, pass down through the first bead strung. Take a small stitch in the suede and weave in the thread.

Step 5 *Making the fringe*

Attach a new 30" (76 cm) length of thread to the bottom edge of the beadwork at one corner. For the shortest drape of beads, string about 22 green size 11 seed beads and pass through a bead on the other side of the lower edge so the loop of beads is centered. String about 35 pale-blue size 15 seed beads and pass the needle around the other loop four or five times. Pass through the beads at the first end of the beadwork, coming out one or two beads closer to the edge. For the second dangle, *string one green size 11 bead, one pale-blue size 15 seed bead, one pale-green oval bead, and one pale-blue size 15 seed bead. Repeat from the asterisk four times.

String one green size 11 bead and pass through beads on the bottom edge of the beadwork so this loop is centered, coming out one or two beads closer to the outer edge. For the last loop of beads string three green size 11 beads, one pale-blue size 15 bead, one small blue drop bead, one pale-blue size 15 bead, three green size 11 beads, one pale-blue size 15 bead, one small blue drop bead, one pale-blue size 15 bead, two green size 11 beads, one green faceted bead, one green size 11 bead, one pale-blue size 15 bead, one blue faceted drop bead. String the same sequence of beads in the opposite direction except omit the blue faceted drop bead. Enter the edge of the beadwork so that the loop is centered and weave in the ends.

Finished Size: approx. 2½" (6.4 cm) round with a 3" (7.6 cm) fringe
Skill Level: Intermediate

Beautiful rich golds, reds and greens are the colors that remind me of the forest and all its changing colors. This brooch features a polymer clay face formed by Corinne Loomer with a mold design by Kimberly Crick from www.theenchantedgallery.com. The colors of clay earth in the face inspired the colors of the pin. Hidden behind the face is a second layer for a favorite photo. Mine is a photo of a place in our local forest reminding me of a fun time I had there exploring and finding frogs with my family. The wood base and polymer clay are both lightweight, making this piece much lighter in weight than it would have been if stone and metal had been used for the main pieces.

MATERIALS

Polymer clay molded face, approx. 1½" (3.8 cm) in diameter
4 g each of green seed beads in sizes 11, 8 and 5
4 g gold-toned size 8 seed beads
4 g metallic burgundy-toned size 11 seed beads
4 g copper-toned size 11 seed beads
4 g brick size 15 seed beads
4 g terra cotta size 15 seed beads
4 g copper-colored charlottes
18 green 5 mm spacer beads
9 gold-toned size 5 seed beads
9 brick-colored 4 mm x 6 mm faceted rondelle beads
5 yellow-gold 5 mm pearls
1 metal gold-toned 8 mm four-sided leaf bead
1 green 3 mm x 6 mm fire-polished bead
1 metal gold-toned 3 mm leaf charm
5 green-and-gold 13 mm center-drilled tulip beads
4 green-and-gold 13 mm side-drilled leaf beads
Suede backing material for polymer face, 2" x 2" (5 cm x 5 cm) square
Thin round wooden disc, 2" (5 cm) diameter, approx. 1⁄16" (0.2 cm) thick
Backing material and suede for wooden disc, 2½" x 2½" (6.4 cm 6.4 cm) square
Round photo, 7⁄8" (2.2 cm)
Size B beading thread
Size 12 beading needle
Pin back
Pencil
Thick white glue

wood nymph secret forest brooch

Beading the Polymer Clay Face

Step 1 *Encasing the face with beads*

Center the polymer clay face on the smaller backing material and draw around it on the backing material with the pencil. Remove the polymer clay face. Thread the needle with a 40" (102 cm) length of thread, tie a knot near the tail and come up from the back of the backing material on the pencil line. Work one row of running stitch with one bead in each stitch and each stitch spaced one bead's width away, using the size 11 metallic burgundy beads (Figure 1).

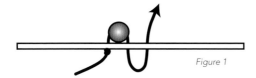

Figure 1

Work two rows of peyote stitch (Figure 2). Place the polymer clay face in the circle of beads (you can use a small amount of thick white glue to hold the face in place or hold it in place as you work). Continue around in peyote stitch, changing to the size 15 brick-colored seed beads, then the terra cotta-colored seed beads, closing the beadwork closely around the face.

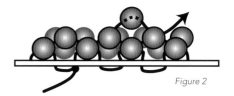

Figure 2

Step 2 *Finishing with the suede backing*

Cut the backing material close to the finished beadwork. Cut the smaller piece of suede to the same size. Glue the suede to the backing material in the center only, using a very small amount of glue, just enough to hold it in place. Let dry. Thread a 24" (61 cm) length of thread with the beading needle and tie a knot at the tail end. Make a small stitch in the backing material to anchor the thread and hide the tail between the backing material and the suede. String one gold-toned size 8 seed bead, one copper-toned size 11 seed bead and one gold-toned size 8 seed bead, make a small stitch through the suede and backing material and pass back through the last bead strung. *String one copper-toned size 11 seed bead and one gold-toned size 8 seed bead, make a small stitch through the suede about one bead's width away and pass back through the gold-toned size 8 seed bead (Figure 3). Repeat from asterisk around.

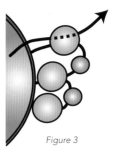

Figure 3

When you get near the beginning, space your stitches so you will end up with no gaps in the beadwork. For the last stitch, string one copper-toned size 11 seed bead and pass down through the first gold-toned size 8 seed bead strung. Do not weave in end.

Step 3 *Adding detail beading along border*

Take a small stitch in the suede and pass through the next three beads in the round, *string one copper-colored charlotte, pass through the next three beads in the round (Figure 4). Repeat from asterisk around. Pass through the next copper-colored charlotte. Weave in ends. Set aside.

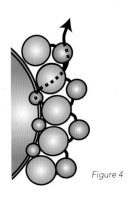

Figure 4

Beading the Wood Base

Step 4 *Stitching the base row*

Using a small amount of glue, glue the wooden disk to the center of the remaining backing material. Let dry. Thread a 40" (102 cm) length of thread with the beading needle and tie a knot near the tail. Come up from the back of the backing material close to the wood disk. Using the metallic burgundy size 11 seed beads, string three beads. Enter the backing material about one bead's width away, next to the edge of the

wood disk. *Pass back up through the backing material about one bead's width away, string two beads, then pass back down through the backing material another bead's width away. Repeat from asterisk around the wooden disk.

Step 5 *Closing the bezel row around the wooden disk*

Pass up through the first two beads again. Working with the green size 8 seed beads *string one bead and pass through the second bead of the next three-bead set (Figure 5). Repeat from asterisk around the cabochon. Work the next rounds in peyote stitch, using the gold-toned size 8 seed beads for the next two rows. Slide the photo into place, then work two more rows of peyote stitch, using the copper-toned size 11 seed beads. Weave in ends.

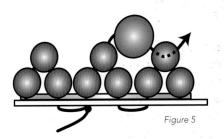

Figure 5

continued on next page…

Finishing

Step 6 *Finishing with the suede backing*

Cut the backing material close to the finished beadwork. Using the permanent glue, attach the pin back to the upper center back of the beadwork. Let dry. Place the remaining piece of suede over the back of the beadwork and mark the ends of the pin back. Cut a small slit at the marking and slide the suede over the pin back. Glue the suede to the backing material in the center only, using a very small amount of glue, just enough to hold it in place. Let dry. Trim the suede to the size of the beadwork. Thread a 30" (76 cm) length of thread with the beading needle and tie a knot at the tail end. Make a small stitch in the backing material to anchor the thread and hide the tail between the backing material and the suede. String one green size 5 seed bead, one metallic burgundy size 11 seed bead and one green size 5 seed bead, make a small stitch through the suede and backing material and pass back through the last bead strung. *String one metallic burgundy size 11 seed bead and one green size 5 seed bead, make a small stitch through

the suede and backing material about one bead's width away and pass back through the green size 5 seed bead. Repeat from asterisk around. When you get near the beginning, space your stitches so you will end up with no gaps in the beadwork. For the last stitch, string one metallic burgundy size 11 seed bead and pass down through the first green size 5 seed bead strung. Do not weave in end.

Step 7 *Hinging the pieces together*

Place the beaded polymer face over the beaded wood disk and find two gold beads on the face that are each less than ½" (1.3 cm) away from the center top and that roughly line up with two green size 8 beads on the wooden disk. Mark with a contrasting thread. Anchor a 24" (61 cm) length of thread near the top of the beadwork on the polymer face by weaving in and out of the finished beadwork, ending near one of the marked gold beads. Pass in and out of the beads on the face and the disk until they are firmly joined together at the hinge beads. Weave in ends.

Step 8 *Making the dangle to open the hinge*

Anchor a 12" (30 cm) length of thread near the bottom of the beadwork on the polymer face by weaving in and out of the finished beadwork, ending at the center bottom on one of the metallic burgundy bead rows. String two metallic burgundy beads, the four-sided metal leaf bead, one metallic burgundy bead, the green fire-polished bead and one metallic burgundy bead. Then pass through the loop of the leaf charm. Pass back up through all the beads and anchor the thread in the beadwork along the polymer face, weaving in and out of several beads so the weight of the dangle isn't all on just one or two beads. Weave around so that the thread is coming out of a bead next to the dangle, then pass back through the dangle beads and charm and back up to the face to strengthen the dangle. Weave in ends.

Step 9 *Making the fringe*

String a 60" (152 cm) length of thread through the center bottom green size 5 bead on the wooden disk, pulling the thread only half way through (Figure 14). String one green size 8 seed bead, 12 metallic burgundy size 11 seed beads, one gold-toned size 8 seed bead, two copper-toned size 11 seed beads, one gold-toned size 8 seed bead, one gold-toned size 5 seed bead, one gold-toned size 8 seed bead, two copper-toned size 11 seed beads, one gold-toned size 8 seed bead, 15 green size 11 seed beads, one green spacer, one faceted brick bead, one green spacer, one tulip, one pearl, and three terra cotta size 15 seed beads. Skip the last three beads and pass back up through all the other beads and through the green size 5 bead. Snug up the thread, adjusting the three terra cotta beads into a triangle shape. Pass down through the next green size 5 bead. String the same sequence but use two fewer metallic burgundy beads and string three terra cotta beads, one leaf bead and three terra cotta beads, instead of the tulip, pearl and three terra cotta beads. Then pass back up through all the other beads strung. Repeat the pattern for three more dangles, always stringing two fewer metallic burgundy beads than the previous dangle (12, 10, 8, 6, 4) and alternating the tulip ending and the leaf ending. Repeat the same process with the other end of the thread in the opposite direction from the center dangle. Weave in the ends.

glossary

Backing Material: *A substance placed on the back side of a cabochon to aid in beading around the cabochon. Backing material is usually a non-woven stiff fabric which is easy to sew through and doesn't fray at the edges. After the cabochon is beaded in place, the backing material is then covered with a piece of synthetic or natural suede or leather and a final row of beading.*

Cab: *Slang term for cabochon.*

Cabochon: *Usually a stone or piece of fused glass that is flat on the bottom and rounded on the top.*

Charlottes: *Round seed beads that are ground flat on one side so they randomly catch and reflect light.*

Clasp: *A component in jewelry making that holds the ends of a bracelet or necklace together. Clasps are usually made of metal, though they can also be made of beads, buttons or other materials.*

Cylinder Beads: *Beads shaped like small cylinders, with straight sides and relatively large holes.*

Dangle: *One hanging strand of beads. It can be a solitary design element, or an element of fringe.*

Earring Wire: *A shaped piece of wire with a small loop at the bottom to add a decorative element for an earring.*

End Cap Beads: *Beads shaped like a bowl used to cover the end of round beads.*

Faceted Beads: *Beads that are ground flat on one or more sides, creating facets.*

Findings: *Components used in jewelry making such as clasps, jump rings, or earring wires.*

Focal Bead: *A bead that is larger and more decorative in relation to the other beads in the piece.*

Fused Glass: *Glass that is layered, then heated in a kiln until it melts together. It can be made into cabochons, beads or other items.*

Fringe: *A collection of dangles stitched next to each other in a row.*

Granny Knot: *A knot made by passing one end of thread around another end, then repeating the same motion again. This knot tends to slide undone.*

Half-hitch Knot: *A simple knot made by making a small stitch around a thread or through fabric, then pulling the stitch almost all the way through, then passing the needle through the loop before the stitch is pulled tight. Half hitch knots help secure a thread in place.*

Jump Ring: *A metal loop of wire used in jewelry making to link items together.*

Nymo: *The brand name of a nylon thread used often in beadwork.*

Pressed Glass Beads: *Beads that have been formed into shape by being pressed into a mold. They can be simple shapes, such as a triangle, or more complex such as leaf or flower shapes.*

Quilter's Knot: *A knot made by winding the tail end of a threaded needle around the needle, then pulling the needle through, creating a knot.*

Seed Beads: *Small doughnut-shaped beads.*

Spacer Beads: *Beads that are generally like discs, shorter through the hole than from side to side. They are often made of metal and are used in a pattern separating other beads.*

Square Knot: *A knot made by passing one end of thread around another end, then repeating the process in the opposite direction. This makes a sturdy knot that doesn't easily slide undone.*

Swarovski Crystals: *A brand name for high-quality leaded glass faceted beads and decorative leaded glass items.*

Turnaround Bead: *In fringe or dangles, the bead or beads at the end of the strand of beads that you skip before passing back through all the beads to create the dangle.*

Synthetic Suede: *A non-woven synthetic material resembling animal suede. Synthetic suede, also commonly called Ultrasuede, is easier to sew through than animal suede.*

projects / resources

I encourage you to always look locally for your supplies. I feel it is important to support your local bead stores, so you can always have the option to see and touch your beads before you buy. Following is a list of manufacturers and internet sources I used to make these projects in case you can't find them locally, or if you want to ask your local store to carry them.

BACKING MATERIALS

www.lacysstiffstuff.com

BEADS AND SUPPLIES

Creative Castle
www.creativecastle.com
(877) 232-3748

BUTTONS

Blue Moon Button Art
www.bluemoonbuttons.com
(970) 884-5256

Gita Maria
www.gitamaria.com

JHB International
www.buttons.com
(303) 751-8100

Susan Clarke Originals
www.susanclarkeoriginals.com

FACE MOLDS

Kimberly Crick
www.theenchantedgallery.com

Bead Your Way to Beautiful Jewelry

The Complete Guide to Beading Techniques
30 Decorative Projects
by Jane Davis

This complete volume of beading techniques is filled with gorgeous photos of antique and contemporary beadwork. Features 30 step-by-step projects.

Softcover • 8¼ x 10⅞ • 160 pages
100 illus. • 150 color photos
Item# BEHME • $24.95

Create Your Own Bling
Add Glamour to Your Favorite Accessories
by Ilene Branowitz

Transform basic bags and accessories into bling beauties, including snappy cell phone cases and handbags, using inexpensive acrylic rhinestones, second-hand bags and the instructions in this innovative book.

Softcover • 8¼ x 10⅞ • 96 pages
150 color photos
Item# Z0381 • $19.99

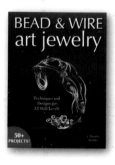

Bead & Wire Art Jewelry
Techniques & Designs for all Skill Levels
by J. Marsha Michler

Incorporates step-by-step instructions and more than 250 detailed color photos and illustrations to demonstrate wirework techniques including beading, hammering, wrapping and coiling, to create more than 50 exciting accessories.

Softcover • 8¼ x 10⅞ • 128 pages
250 color photos and illus.
Item# EBWJ • $21.99

Button Jewelry
Over 25 Original Designs for Necklaces, Earrings, Bracelets and More
By Sara Withers

This stylish book shows how vintage and new buttons can be combined with all kinds of beads and pearls to create a wide range of original pieces from necklaces to earrings.

Softcover • 8½ x 8½ • 128 pages
250 color photos
Item# Z0402 • $22.99

Creating Lampwork Beads for Jewelry
by Karen J. Leonardo

Explore the world of lampwork beading through the 200 color photos and instructions in this unique guide, while you discover the ability to create lampwork beads and 16 related jewelry designs.

Softcover • 8¼ x 10⅞ • 144 pages
75 b&w illus. • 225 color photos and illus.
Item# Z0975 • $24.99

kp **krause publications**
An imprint of F+W Publications, Inc.

P.O. Box 5009, Iola, WI 54945-5009
www.krausebooks.com

Order directly from the publisher by calling
800-258-0929 M-F 8 am - 5 pm

Online at www.krausebooks.com, or from booksellers and craft and fabric shops nationwide.

Please reference **offer CRB7** with all direct-to-publisher orders.